BROKEN ARROW

AMERICA'S FIRST LOST NUCLEAR WEAPON

NORMAN S. LEACH

Red Deer PRESS

5 4 3 2 1

Published by Red Deer Press
A Fitzhenry & Whiteside Company
1512, 1800 4 Street SW
Calgary AB T2S 2S5
www.reddeerpress.com
www.fitzhenry.ca

Credits

Cover and text design by Jacquie Morris and Delta Embree
Front cover images courtesy USAF; backcover (top) unattributed – Norman Leach (middle)
Doug Davidge (bottom) Norman Leach.
Printed and bound in Canada

Acknowledgements

Red Deer Press acknowledges the support of the Canada Council for the Arts.
Financial support also provided by Government of Canada through the
Book Publishing Industry Development Program (BPIDP).

Canada Council for the Arts   Conseil des Arts du Canada

Library and Archives Canada Cataloguing in Publication

Leach, Norman, 1963–
Broken arrow : America's first lost nuclear weapon / Norman Leach.

Includes bibliographical references.
ISBN 978-0-88995-348-2

1. Nuclear weapons—Accidents—British Columbia—Pacific Coast.
2. Aircraft accidents—British Columbia—Pacific Coast—History—20th century.
3. Airplanes, Military—Accidents—British Columbia—Pacific Coast—History—20th century.
4. Atomic bomb—United States—History.
I. Title.

TL553.53.C3L42 2007   363.17'990916433   C2006-905472-X

THIS BOOK COULD NOT HAVE HAPPENED

without the patience, help and love of my wife,

Maritza, and my daughters, Stephanie and Chelsea.

They were there through all the long days and

even longer nights of research and writing.

THIS BOOK IS DEDICATED TO THEM.

Contents

Acknowledgements

THIS BOOK COULD NOT HAVE BEEN WRITTEN WITHOUT THE ASSISTANCE of a great number of people. I especially wish to acknowledge the assistance of my sister Sheila Leach-Dougherty, who helped me understand what it is to be a pilot, and Judith Martinez, Cynthia Hernandez and Maritza Leach, who helped with the footnoting and research. The U.S. Air Force provided open access to research materials, and the National Museum of the U.S. Air Force made available many of the photos in this book.

The assistance of the 7th Bomb Wing B-36 Association was indispensable. The association was formed in September 1981, and its members include veterans of B-36 duty in the 7th and 11th Bomb Wings at Carswell Air Force Base, Fort Worth, Texas. Special thanks are extended to the association's historian, Lt. Col. Frank F. Kleinwechter, Jr., USAF (ret) and to assistant historian, Don Pyeatt. Also, Doug Davidge kindly permitted the use of his photos of Ship 2075's crash site.

This book was made much better through the hard work, diligence and mentorship of my editor, Dennis Johnson, assisted by Mark Giles. A hearty thank you.

Finally, a thank you to the men who flew the B-36 bomber for the Strategic Air Command during a time when the free world was at risk. We owe them all a real debt of gratitude.

Wherever possible Internet sites have been cited rather than original archival sources to make source documents more accessible to readers.

Introduction

By early 1950 the world, still recoiling from the horrors of World War II, had again become a very dangerous place. The communists in the Soviet Union were firmly rooted in power and were threatening to push ever deeper into the rest of Europe. The Chinese under Mao Tse Tung had defeated the Nationalists and were in the process of establishing a Communist regime throughout China. To the Western world it appeared the communists would one day soon control much if not the whole of Europe and Asia.

Each and every day the men of the Strategic Air Command (SAC) climbed aboard their long-range bombers and flew mission after mission, preparing for the war they believed to be inevitable. They had no reason to doubt their commander, the legendary General Curtis LeMay, when he told them they formed the free world's first line of defense against communist aggression.

By 1950 the giant new B-36 bomber was SAC's most potent strategic weapon—a long-range bomber that could deliver nuclear weapons deep within Soviet territory and escape if not undetected, then at least unscathed. SAC crews had a love-hate relationship with the bomber. It was cutting-edge technology, but anyone who flew it knew it was unreliable, with crashes usually being fatal.

On 13 February 1950, as Captain Theodore Schreier and his fellow crew members climbed aboard their B-36, Ship 2075, and took off from Eielson Air Force Base in the fading light of an Alaskan winter, they had any number of reasons to suspect that their twenty-hour training flight to San Francisco and then back home to Fort Worth, Texas, could turn out to be anything but routine. The aircraft had known and unresolved maintenance issues, and was largely untested in the brutal winter conditions of Alaska. For another, the Mark IV Fat Man nuclear

Air and maintenance crews pose in front of a B-36, America's first long-range nuclear bomber. COURTESY USAF

bomb hanging in bomb bay No. 1 was pushing to the limit LeMay's requirement that training be "as close to war as it gets." Their flight would be the first to test the Fat Man's weapon systems aboard America's latest and most lethal bomber.

Six hours later, flying into a gale and rapidly losing altitude off Canada's west coast, Ship 2075 was in peril, having lost three engines to fire. The crew was left no option but to jettison and destroy the atomic bomb over foreign waters, send the top-secret bomber on autopilot out to crash into the sea and bail out over a rugged Canadian island. As the United States Air Force would eventually learn, things did not go as planned.

At midnight on Valentine's Day 1950, Ship 2075 and Captain Ted Schreier would become the center of a mystery that would last for over fifty years. What was the true fate of the Mark IV Fat Man nuclear bomb that Ship 2075 carried? What was real location of the crash site of the B-36? And, most importantly, what really happened to Captain Theodore Schreier?

CHAPTER ONE

America and the Bomb

For many North Americans in the early 1950s, the Cold War divided the globe into neat halves—goodness and democracy on the one side, evil and communism on the other. Men like Captain Theodore Schreier of the United States Strategic Air Command (SAC) traced the divide of this undeclared conflict between East and West while flying America's first long-range nuclear bomber. A pilot, navigator and atomic weaponeer, Schreier was among the earliest of the cold warriors. He patrolled America's first line of defense against the threat posed by an ever-encroaching Soviet Union, which seemed poised to engulf post–World War II Europe.

Main gate, Carswell Air Force Base, Fort Worth, Texas.
COURTESY GLEN LOVEALL AND DON PYEATT

Schreier had piloted bombers in the European theater during World War II. By early January 1950, he was stationed at Carswell Air Force Base (AFB) in Fort Worth, Texas. For Schreier, the Communist "Red Menace" loomed as a very real danger. The fact that he had been called back to active duty from the reserves was proof enough of the fragile peace that followed the war. His morning newspaper carried almost daily stories of the Communist threat to the free world. In the next month, he was scheduled to crew on the first training mission to carry a nuclear weapon. Not that he could tell anyone—not even his devoted wife, Jean. Soviet spies were believed to be everywhere. Schreier and his fellow SAC airmen were on red alert every day of their active service. Nuclear war with the Soviets seemed only a matter of time.

NEW AGE USHERED
HIROSHIMA IS TARGET
FIRST ATOMIC BOMB DROPPED ON JAPAN

New York Times 7 August 1945

The first news of the atomic bomb Schreier would eventually carry heralded the end of World War II. Before the bomb was news, it was a secret. As early as 1940, U.S. scientists and military planners were designing a powerful new weapon, code-named the Manhattan Project, conceived as a way to end to the war in Europe. But it was not until 16 July 1945, almost three months after VE Day, that the first nuclear test device blasted a crater in the desert near Los Alamos, New Mexico, and raised a mushroom-shaped cloud of radioactive dust into the sky. Frightening in its power, the new secret weapon was too late to be used in Europe but was just in time to help end the war in the Pacific.

U.S. President Harry S. Truman personally approved the dropping of nuclear weapons on Japan. Truman's stated intention in ordering the bombings was "to bring about a quick resolution of the war by inflicting destruction, and instilling fear of further destruction, that was sufficient to cause Japan to surrender." Credible U.S. military estimates predicted that the invasion of the Japanese home islands would cost one million American casualties, many of those in brutal and protracted hand-to-hand combat. Truman balked at the price.

U.S. military planners selected Hiroshima as the first target for the potent new weapon. The central Japanese city had some military camps nearby and was a communications center, storage point and assembly area for troops. More importantly, Hiroshima was one of the few Japanese cities that General Curtis LeMay's bomb group had not yet carpet- and fire-bombed. Planners sought an undamaged city on which to accurately measure the destructive power of the atomic bomb.

On 6 August 1945, the *Enola Gay*, along with two sister B-29 bombers, lumbered into the air from Tinian airbase in the west Pacific. Nestled in the *Enola Gay*'s bomb bay was the Little Boy atomic device. Six hours ahead lay Hiroshima. At 7:00 AM that morning, Japanese early warning radar began tracking the B-29s. Instantly, radio broadcasts from Nagasaki in the south to Nagoya in the north started to shut down. Anti-aircraft gun crews prepared for a possible attack and the expected rain of incendiary bombs.

Because U.S. bombing raids typically approached at much lower altitudes, the B-29's high-altitude approach lulled the Japanese defenders into a false sense of security. Approximately an hour later, a radar operator in Hiroshima concluded that the flight of enemy warplanes was probably only a scouting or reconnaissance mission and signaled the all-clear. Radio broadcasts informed people that it was safe to leave bomb shelters but to be prepared to return if the B-29s were actually spotted.

To describe the decision as a mistake would be to understate the misfortune of its impact. Only fifteen minutes later, the *Enola Gay* began its bombing run over the city of 255,000. Right on target, the bomber dropped its payload over the center of Hiroshima. A gravity bomb containing 130 pounds of Uranium-235, it exploded at an altitude of about 2,000 feet with a blast equivalent to 13,000 tons of TNT. Within the immediate blast radius of one mile, virtually every structure was leveled. From ground zero the blast propelled a supersonic shockwave that raced across the city at 1,500 feet per second— faster than the speed of sound— collapsing buildings and trapping thousands in the furnace-like heat. Tile and glass melted. Combustible materials vaporized to ash. As far as two miles from ground zero, the intense heat caused severe burns to victims. The ensuing firestorm destroyed another 4.4 square miles of the city. Eighty thousand people were killed instantly, many literally evaporated. Another 70,000 died over time from the effects of radiation.

Three days later, Army Air Corps crews loaded America's second-generation nuclear bomb, the Fat Man, aboard a B-29 Superfortress named *Bockscar.* Its target: Kokura, Japan. Bad weather obscured the city, and the crews diverted to their secondary target, Nagasaki.

The Japanese repeated the mistake of Hiroshima. At 7:50 AM military authorities in Nagasaki sounded an air raid but gave the all-clear an hour later. Just after 11:00 AM a break in the clouds allowed *Bockscar* to drop the Fat Man over the city's industrial valley. With its core of 14 pounds of Plutonium-239, the bomb exploded 1,540 feet above the city. Again, the immediate blast area was one mile in circumference, and the ensuing firestorm multiplied the destruction. Seventy thousand perished. The nuclear bombs that devastated Hiroshima and Nagasaki blew open the curtain for the drama of the nuclear age and set the stage for Captain Ted Schreier's entrance a few years later.

DECISIONS AT YALTA POSE VITAL TEST FOR AMERICA

New York Times 18 February 1945

Eight months before the mushroom clouds over Japan heralded a new world order, the war in Europe was quickly drawing to a close. Everyone, with the possible exception of Adolf Hitler, knew the end was inevitable. In the Pacific, the Japanese were proving more tenacious, defending their conquests island by island at a terrible cost to U.S. servicemen. With Germany defeated, America threw all her industrial and military might against the island country.

Throughout the war in Europe, the alliance between the Soviet Union, the United States, Great Britain and the other Allied powers was at best uneasy. Even before the European war ended, generals such as American George S. Patton were openly discussing the next war in which the Soviet Union and the West would square off. Patton recognized that Joseph Stalin would never allow Germany to threaten the Soviet Union again and that he would advance the Soviet sphere of influence over Eastern Europe to provide a buffer zone against attack. As early as 1943, the Soviet Union established the Soviet Alliance System that allowed Stalin to gain military and political control over Eastern European countries after the war ended.

The Soviets had ample cause to doubt the Allies. As the war raged in Europe, they repeatedly pleaded with the Allies to open a second front to relieve the pressure on the Russian front, where cities such as Stalingrad lay under siege and the death toll was staggering. The U.S. lost 415,000 servicemen in World War II, almost all on active military duty, but the Soviets lost 25 million, mostly civilians. For two years the Allies refused, claiming insufficient manpower and resources. Hitler's dilemma in trying to wage a war on two fronts was a lesson not lost on Allied military planners.

Six months before the bombing of Hiroshima, the leaders of the United States, Britain and the Soviet Union met at the Yalta Conference to partition the soon-to-be-defeated Germany. U.S. planners recognized that Soviet plans for Eastern Europe were inflexible. Germany would fall under an occupational regime, while the states sandwiched between the Soviet Union and Germany—Estonia, Latvia, Lithuania, Poland, Czechoslovakia, Romania, Hungary, Yugoslavia, Bulgaria and Albania—would become the Soviet's buffer zone. Churchill and Roosevelt reluctantly agreed to Soviet control over the countries on the Soviet's western border.

After Germany surrendered on 24 May 1945, the world became aware that the Soviet Union was intent on conquering non-Communist opposition groups in Eastern Europe and building up a standing force of over one million Red Army soldiers. In the West the Allies were intent on quickly demobilizing their armies, navies and air forces. If the Soviets attacked, the West had neither the heart nor the resources to fight another land war in Europe. The geopolitical conditions that would divide the globe during the Cold War began to coalesce.

TRUMAN SUPPORTS McMAHON ATOM BILL
CALLS FOR MONOPOLY BY GOVERNMENT

New York Times 3 February 1946

After the end of the war in the Pacific, Truman struggled with his decision to drop nuclear bombs on Japan. He wrote that he believed the decision had been justified but that he hoped no president would ever have to make a similar choice. In Washington the atomic bomb provoked intense debates among politicians and bureaucrats. Who should control the new weapon and the associated technology—

civilians or the military? As early as September 1944, a proposal presented to Secretary of War Henry L. Stimson called for the establishment of "a civilian twelve-member atomic energy commission, with four members representing the military services, that would control not only large-scale production but also research involving minute amounts of *nuclear* material."

On 1 August 1946, almost a year after the bombing of Hiroshima and Nagasaki, Truman signed the McMahon Act, placing control of the U.S. nuclear arsenal under civilian authority. Known officially as the Atomic Energy Act of 1946, the legislation created the United States Atomic Energy Commission (AEC) to control all nuclear weapons then in the army's possession. Under the act, "the commission was to be the 'exclusive owner' of production facilities but could let contracts to operate them." The act also contained the provision for the president "from time to time" to direct the commission to deliver "weapons to the armed forces for such use as [the president] deems necessary in the interest of national defense."All nuclear assets were transferred to the Atomic Energy Commission at midnight, 31 December 1946.

The military found itself in a paradox. They were to use nuclear weapons to deter the emerging Soviet threat but did not have any nuclear weapons in their possession.

BRITON SPEAKS OUT
DISTINGUISHED VISITORS AT WESTMINSTER COLLEGE
CHURCHILL HITS RUSSIAN POLICIES

New York Times 6 March 1946

In early 1946 Sir Winston Churchill, former Prime Minster of Great Britain, traveled with President Harry Truman to deliver a speech at Westminster College, Fulton, Missouri. The town had a population of only 7,000, but 40,000 turned out to hear the great orator.

With World War II not yet a year in the past, both the U.S. and British governments were intent on returning to peacetime economies and were content to see the Soviets exercising the conditions of the Yalta Agreement. The Fulton speech went beyond Yalta and introduced a new dynamic that rattled any sense of growing postwar complacency. Churchill spoke in solemn tones of the new threat to Western European democracies:

> From Stettin in the Baltic to Trieste in the Adriatic, an iron curtain has descended across the Continent. Behind that line lie all the capitals of the ancient states of Central and Eastern Europe. Warsaw, Berlin, Prague, Vienna, Budapest, Belgrade, Bucharest and Sofia, all these famous cities and the populations around them lie in what I must call the Soviet sphere, and all are subject in one form or another, not only to Soviet influence but to a very high and, in many cases, increasing measure of control from Moscow. Athens alone—Greece with its immortal glories—is free to decide its future at an election under British, U.S. and French observation. The Russian-dominated Polish Government has been encouraged to make enormous and wrongful inroads upon Germany, and mass expulsions of millions of Germans on a scale grievous and undreamed-of are now taking place. An attempt is being made by the Russians in Berlin to build up a quasi-Communist party in their zone of Occupied Germany by showing special favors to groups of left-wing German leaders.
>
> From what I have seen of our Russian friends and Allies during the war, I am convinced that there is nothing they admire so much as strength, and there is nothing for which they have less respect than for weakness, especially military weakness. For that reason the old doctrine of a balance of power is unsound. We cannot afford, if we can help it, to work on narrow margins, offering temptations to a trial of strength. If the Western Democracies stand together in strict adherence to the principles of the United Nations Charter, their influence for furthering those principles will be immense and no one is likely to molest them. If, however, they become divided or falter in their duty and if these all-important years are allowed to slip away then indeed catastrophe may overwhelm us all.

The speech put a name to the growing divide between the Soviets and the West, and overnight the Iron Curtain became the metaphoric frontline that men like Schreier patrolled for the Strategic Air

Command. Many historians consider Churchill's so-called Iron Curtain speech, which portrayed the Soviets as expansionist and evil, as the beginning of the Cold War in the public's perception.

SOVIET POLICE TIED TO SPIES IN CANADA

New York Times 23 March 1946

Igor Sergeyevich Gouzenko, born in the Soviet Union and trained as a cipher clerk, was stationed in Ottawa, Ontario, where he coded and deciphered messages for Soviet intelligence. The nature of his work gave him access to Soviet espionage activities in the West.

In 1945 Gouzenko received word that he was to be transferred back to the Soviet Union. He and his family had become accustomed to their lifestyle in the West, and a return to the drudgery and oppression of the Soviet economic and political regime was not inviting. In an effort to remain in Canada, Gouzenko slipped out of the Soviet Embassy on 5 September 1945 carrying a booty of code books and deciphering materials he hoped to trade for freedom in the West.

His first stop was the Royal Canadian Mounted Police (RCMP), who were responsible for counterespionage activities in Canada. The RCMP turned him away, refusing to believe their former wartime ally would spy on Canada. Gouzenko didn't fare any better with the *Ottawa Journal*, where the night editor gave no credence to a crazy Russian claiming to be a spy. At the Justice Ministry, no one was on duty. The Soviet cipher clerk wandered the streets of Canada's capital, clutching the key that could unlock many secrets of Soviet ambition, trying in vain to use it to open a door to his freedom.

By the following day, Gouzenko was terrified that his controllers at the Soviet embassy would be hunting for him and the stolen codebooks. He was right to be afraid. Hiding in a neighbor's apartment across the hall from his own, Gouzenko and his family listened as Soviet agents broke into their apartment and tore it apart, looking for the missing spy documents.

The next day Gouzenko approached the RCMP one more time. This time they were ready to listen. As a result of the Gouzenko defection, the RCMP arrested a total of thirty-nine Canadian suspects, eighteen of whom were eventually convicted. They included Fred Rose, the only

Communist member of parliament in the Canadian House of Commons, and Sam Carr, the Communist Party's national organizer in Canada.

Gouzenko eventually testified at a Royal Commission of Inquiry, alerting other countries to the Soviet spies in their backyard. As a result of Gouzenko's testimony, Alan Nunn May, Klaus Fuchs, and Julius and Ethel Rosenberg were exposed and arrested. Out of fear of Soviet reprisal, Gouzenko and his family were given new identities by the Canadian government. His cache of secrets exposed the Allies' wartime ally as an enemy.

BARUCH'S SPEECH AT OPENING SESSIONS OF U.N. ATOMIC ENERGY COMMISSION

New York Times 15 June 1946

When President Truman announced that America and her allies had harnessed the power of the atom, he promised it would not be used for weapons alone. "Science, which gave us this dread power," he declared, "shows that it can be made a giant help to humanity, but science does not show us how to prevent its baleful use. So we have been appointed to obviate that peril by finding a meeting of the minds and the hearts of our peoples. Only in the will of mankind lies the answer."

Bernard M. Baruch, the U.S. representative to the United Nations Atomic Energy Commission, proposed the establishment of an Atomic Energy Development Authority (AEDA) that would "control the development and use of atomic energy, beginning from the mining stage and including the development and implementation of atomic energy and its uses." The plan called for the elimination of nuclear weapons and for inspection teams to ensure the signatories followed the rules. In exchange for an international treaty on the use of nuclear power, the United States agreed to turn over all nuclear weapons in its possession to the AEDA.

Discussions dragged on between the Soviet Union and the United States with each, ultimately, agreeing to disagree. The Baruch Plan was never signed. However, from 1946 onward, Americans maintained that they had attempted in good faith to ban nuclear weapons, and they cast blame on the Soviets for precipitating the nuclear arms race.

AMERICA'S GLOBAL PLANNER

New York Times 13 July 1947

In February 1946 the first U.S. military strategy to counter the Soviet threat to Europe emerged when George Frost Kennan, *charge d'affaires* at the U.S. Embassy in Moscow, sat down at his desk to dictate what would become one of the most important documents of the Cold War. Responding to an urgent request by the State Department for clarification of Soviet conduct, Kennan composed what would become known as the Long Telegram, an 8,000-word appraisal of the Soviets. Kennan argued that the Soviets were

> . . . a political force committed fanatically to the belief that with United States there can be no permanent *modus vivendi,* that it is desirable and necessary that the internal harmony of our society be disrupted, our traditional way of life be destroyed, the international authority of our state be broken, if Soviet power is to be secure. . . . In addition, *Soviet power* has an elaborate and far flung apparatus for exertion of its influence in other countries, an apparatus of amazing flexibility and versatility, managed by people whose experience and skill in underground methods are presumably without parallel in history. . . .
>
> I would like to record my conviction that the problem is within our power to solve—and that without recourse to any general military conflict. And in support of this conviction there are certain observations of a more encouraging nature I should like to make:
>
> 1. Soviet power, unlike that of Hitlerite Germany, is neither schematic nor adventuristic. It does not work by fixed plans. It does not take unnecessary risks. Impervious to logic of reason, it is highly sensitive to logic of force: For this reason it can easily withdraw—and usually does—when strong resistance is encountered at any point. Thus, if the adversary has sufficient force and makes clear his readiness to use it, he rarely has to do so. If situations are properly handled there need be no prestige engaging showdowns.
> 2. Gauged against [the] Western world as a whole, [the]

> Soviets are still by far the weaker force. Thus, their success will really depend on [the] degree of cohesion, firmness and vigor which [the] Western world can muster. . . .
>
> For these reasons I think we may approach calmly and with good heart [the] problem of how to deal with Russia. . . . Our first step must be to apprehend . . . the nature of the movement with which we are dealing. We must study it with [the] same courage, detachment, objectivity, and same determination not to be emotionally provoked or unseated by it, with which [a] doctor studies [an] unruly and unreasonable individual.
>
> Much depends on [the] health and vigor of our own society. World communism is like [a] malignant parasite which feeds only on diseased tissue. . . .
>
> We must formulate and put forward for other nations a much more positive and constructive picture of world we would like to see than we have put forward in [the] past.
>
> Finally we must have courage and self-confidence to cling to our own methods and conceptions of human society. . . .

The Long Telegram succinctly outlined the strategy of containment that would become the cornerstone of U.S. foreign policy toward the communist world for the next fifty years.

TRUMAN DOCTRINE IN ACTION

New York Times 12 November 1947

Influenced by the Kennan telegram and alarmed over Soviet aggression in not just Europe but the Middle East (including activities in Iran, Turkey and Greece), the Truman government found an appropriate political and military response in containment. The policy, known as the Truman Doctrine, declared that the United States was prepared to provide financial aid, equipment or military forces to countries threatened by Communist powers. Truman warned the world that it was "the policy of the United States to support free peoples who are resisting attempted subjugation by armed minorities or by outside pressures." The Truman Doctrine "signaled America's post-war embrace of global leadership and ended its longstanding policy of isolationism."

Truman signed the act into law on 22 May 1947, granting $400 million in military and economic aid to Turkey and Greece. Italy and France were also given a variety of assistance to counter strong Communist movements.

MARSHALL PLAN IS HELD AIMED NOT AT RUSSIA, BUT TO AID PEACE

New York Times 13 November 1947

In 1947 the United States invited countries from across Europe to a meeting to plan the postwar reconstruction of the continent. While the Soviets and their allies were also invited, they declined to attend. The plan called for the United States to provide $13 billion in economic and technical assistance ($130 billion in today's dollars) over a four-year period to aid in the recovery of the European countries that had joined the Organization for European Economic Cooperation. The plan, known as the Marshall Plan (officially the European Recovery Program), was created by William L. Clayton and George F. Kennan (of the Long Telegram) and brokered by George Marshall, the United States Secretary of State.

For most European states, the Marshall Plan was a resounding success. "By the time the plan had come to completion, the economy of every participant state, with the exception of Germany, had grown well past pre-war levels. Over the next two decades Western Europe, as a whole, would enjoy unprecedented growth and prosperity." The Marshall Plan was also responsible for directing Europe along the path toward continental integration.

CZECH REDS SEIZING POWER, OCCUPY SOME MINISTRIES

SOCIALIST PARTY TAKEN OVER

New York Times 25 February 1948

But just as the United States moved to consolidate its influence and to encourage the ascendancy of democracy in western Europe, so too did the USSR seize the opportunity to further its own expansionist ideology. After World War II, Czechoslovakia had elected a democratic government, but the political situation remained highly unstable. The Communist Party, facing an erosion of influence in popular opinion as an election approached, staged a *coup d'etat* that was quietly supported by the Soviet Union.

To control the army, the Communist leader, Svoboda, confined all non-Communist commanders to their quarters. Communist-controlled units were placed on full alert as the coup leaders installed a Moscow-friendly government. The new regime purged the newly renamed Czechoslovak People's Army (CSLA) of "politically unreliable" officers and soldiers, weakening it to the point that the Soviets had to step in with military advisers to stabilize it. Soon the Czechoslovaks, trained and equipped by the Soviets, became a potent military force. By 1950 the CSLA had grown to over 140,000 troops with the goal of 250,000 within a year. To the West, growing Soviet influence in Czechoslovakia was proof positive that Soviet ambitions would not be restrained by the Yalta agreement.

REDS CLAIM VICTORY
2 SUCHOW ARMIES FINISHED, REDS SAY

New York Times 11 January 1949

As the postwar realignment of the globe progressed, political upheavals were not limited to Europe. As peace talks broke down between the Kuomintang, or Chinese Nationalist Party (KMT), and the Communist Party of China (CCP), intense fighting renewed in the Chinese Civil War that had been underway since 1946. Each side received support from the outside. The Communists under Mao Tse Tung received limited support from the Soviets, while the Nationalists under Chiang Kai-Shek received "hundreds of millions of dollars worth of (now-surplus) military supplies and equipment, as well as the airlifting of many Nationalist troops from central China to Manchuria, which Chiang Kai-Shek saw as strategically vital to defend against a communist advance, from the United States."

Ultimately, the Nationalists could not hold Manchuria, and the Communists seized not only the entire region but large numbers of Nationalist troops and equipment as well. For the first time, Mao and his followers had access to the weapons needed to begin the final push against the Nationalists. In January 1949 Beijing fell to the Communists without a fight. On 1 October 1949, Mao Tse Tung proclaimed the People's Republic of China, and a month later almost all of China was under Communist control, taken with very little resistance as the People's Liberation Army rolled south. Chiang Kai-shek, together with 600,000 Nationalist troops and two million Nationalist refugees, retreated to the island of Taiwan and proclaimed the Republic of China.

From the perspective of the West, the Communists were redrawing the world map at an alarming rate.

MOSCOW PROTESTS ATLANTIC TREATY AS U.N. VIOLATION
DECLARES 'OPENLY AGGRESSIVE' ALLIANCE IS AIMED AGAINST SOVIET AND SATELLITES

New York Times 1 April 1949

As the Soviets began to physically withdraw from the European and Asian countries they had occupied, they demanded extensive concessions—oil concessions in Iran and the right to deploy spies from Turkey among them. They supported a Communist revolution in Greece that led to a bloody civil war. These persistent activities, combined with the coup in Czechoslovakia, presented a hostile face to the West. In response, the Brussels Treaty defensively linked Britain, France and the Benelux countries.

As Soviet aggression continued, the West looked for a way to coordinate its response. In April 1949, in accordance with the United Nations Charter, twelve nations—Belgium, Canada, Denmark, France, Great Britain, Iceland, Italy, Luxembourg, the Netherlands, Norway, Portugal and the United States—established the North Atlantic Treaty Organization (NATO). The signatories agreed "to consider an armed attack against any one of them as an attack against all." In December 1950 General Dwight D. Eisenhower became the Supreme Commander of NATO military forces. The West had confirmed to the rest of the world that it would not only support democracy with money but with military might.

SOVIET ACHIEVED THE BOMB QUICKLY

New York Times 24 September 1949

In international politics and espionage, sometimes much hinges not on what is said but what is not. In April 1942 Georgii Flerov, a prominent Soviet physicist, reported to Soviet leader Joseph Stalin that the Americans and British were strangely silent on the question of nuclear fission. Fission had first been discovered and widely reported in 1939. Flerov pointed out that "nothing was being published in the physics journals by Americans, Britains, or Germans and that many of the most prominent physicists in Allied countries seemed not to be publishing at all." Stalin shared Flerov's suspicions but could not commit to a full-scale Soviet nuclear development program as long as the war continued with Nazi Germany. Stalin did, however, launch a limited nuclear program headed by his former chief of security, Lavrentii Beria, with Igor Kurchatiov as its scientific head. The project was moved to the small village of Sarov, which Stalin and Beria erased from maps of the Soviet Union. Secrecy was paramount.

Beria and Kurchatiov recruited spies to accelerate the development of a Soviet nuclear weapon. Beria's agents actively searched for information on the development of the nuclear bomb in both the United States and Great Britain. The gun had sounded for the nuclear arms race, and Beria had no intention of being last to the tape. The Soviet Union needed the atomic bomb quickly, and Beria's spies made it possible. The first test of the Soviet bomb on 29 August 1949, dubbed First Lightning, was a virtual replica of the U.S. Fat Man bomb.

For the West, the Soviet atomic test came as a shock. Only fourteen months before, the Central Intelligence Agency had estimated that the Soviet Union would not have the bomb within five years. Now the West faced not only an aggressive enemy but one armed with nuclear weapons.

FUCHS CASE POSES SECURITY DILEMMA

New York Times 12 February 1950

Emil Julius Klaus Fuchs betrayed the secret of the bomb to the Soviet Union before being arrested on 2 February 1950. Fuchs was a German theoretical physicist who, while attending university in Germany, had joined the Social Democratic Party and then the Communist Party. In 1933 he fled Germany for Bristol, England, where he earned his PhD in physics.

Late 1940s view of Carswell AFB, Fort Worth, Texas, showing B-36 bombers on tarmac. The Consolidated Vultee factory, the B-36's maker, is in the background. COURTESY JACK KERR AND FRANK KLEINWECHTER

When World War II broke out, Fuchs was interned, along with other German nationals, on the Isle of Man, off the coast of England. Later he was moved to Quebec, Canada. In early 1941 university friends and colleagues intervened on his behalf with the British government, and Fuchs was released from confinement. He landed in Edinburgh and was hired to work on the British atomic bomb project.

When Germany invaded the Soviet Union in 1941, Fuchs began to transmit military secrets to the USSR, believing "that the Soviets had a right to know what the United Kingdom (and later the United States) was working on in secret." He would always maintain that he was simply assisting a loyal ally. His spying went undetected, and a year later Fuchs received his British citizenship and promptly signed the Official Secrets Act. In late 1943 Fuchs transferred to Columbia University in New York City to work on the Manhattan Project. Within months he was assigned to the Theoretical Physics Division at Los Alamos, New Mexico, where he witnessed the first operational test of a nuclear weapon.

According to testimony given at his year-and-a-half-long trial, Fuchs passed crucial data that included "the principal theoretical outline for creating a hydrogen bomb and initial drafts for its development, at the stage they were being worked on in England and America as well as the results of the test at Eniwetok Atoll of uranium and plutonium bombs." Further, Fuchs provided "key data on production of Uranium-235. Fuchs revealed that American production was one hundred kilograms of U-235 a month and twenty kilos of plutonium per month." Capable of both idealism and cold calculation, Fuchs almost certainly would have avoided prison had he not volunteered his confession. A month later he was sentenced to fourteen years for breaking the Official Secrets Act and was stripped of his British citizenship. After serving nine years in prison, he defected to East Germany to work on their nuclear program.

Fuchs' betrayal allowed the Soviets to calculate the number of nuclear bombs the Americans had in their arsenal and to conclude that "the United States was not prepared for a nuclear war at the end of the 1940s or even into the early 1950s."

By early 1950 Strategic Air Command personnnel like Captain Theodore Schreier were at the vanguard of American foreign policy and in the crucible of geopolitical forces between East and West. As pilot, navigator and weaponeer, Schreier knew that the order to drop atomic bombs on the Soviet Union could come any day. His job was to get the nuclear bomb to the USSR, drop it right on target and prevent the Soviets from annexing more of Europe. Now that the Soviets had a bomb of their own to muscle the spread of Communism throughout more of Europe and Asia, the aircrews of the Strategic Air Command faced a heightened level of tension. Schreier and his fellow airmen were flying headlong into the storm front of the Cold War.

CHAPTER TWO

The B-36 and the Atomic Bomb

After World War II, war-weary Americans longed to turn their attention to their families and communities, to lives of quietude and plenitude. They wanted new cars with chrome-plated trim, silk stockings, butter—all the things that wartime rationing had denied. They wanted factories producing appliances instead of armaments. Women left the assembly lines and returned to the home. Battle veterans like Ted Schreier, trained in the arts of war, turned their skills to civilian pursuits.

The country had fought wars in both Europe and the Pacific, and had emerged victorious. But the cost had been high. The United States had suffered almost 300,000 combat deaths with another 115,000 deaths due to infection and disease. Another 140,000 combat personnel were officially listed as missing in action and presumed dead. The total number of wounded was over 670,000. In terms of dollars, the war had cost America over $350 billion—a staggering $5 trillion in today's dollars. Movies like *The Best Years of Our Lives* documented both the anxiety and suffering of the losses, and reached out for the promise of peace. But rising tensions between the West and the Soviet Union presented new anxieties, especially with the specter of atomic warfare looming. These anxieties took material shape with the development of the B-36 bomber, soon to be thundering overhead and into history over Canada's Queen Charlotte Sound. World War II bomber pilot Ted Schreier was called out of the cockpit of American Airlines passenger planes and returned to active military service.

Military planners grew more and more concerned as the Soviets pushed farther and farther into Western Europe, yet they knew that the

U.S. public would not endure another costly land war so soon on the heels of the last one. As early as 1946, U.S. military planners predicted that the Soviet Union, with its massive land forces, could invade and conquer all of Europe in less than four weeks. The United States could not rebuild and transport its military to Europe in time to save the continent. A plan to counter the Soviet threat emerged: wholesale destruction of the enemy by nuclear weapons delivered by long-range bombers based in the United States. James Schlesinger, former Secretary of both Defense and Energy, and Director of the CIA, wrote: "The goal for the military might of the United States and its allies since the late forties has been to create an effective structure of deterrence that will preclude outright military assault."

For deterrence to work effectively, the United States needed the means to deliver a prompt and lethal retaliatory blow. The United States had to demonstrate that it held the cards to win at geopolitical poker and was not afraid to lay them down. As one commentator put it, deterrence became "a façade." During the Cold War nuclear weapons became the winning hand for the United States to "deter a massive conventional attack against NATO by the Soviet Union and its allies."

In 1946 Bernard Brodie, a naval strategist, summed up how nuclear weapons had changed the world of military strategy:

> The first and most vital step in any American security program for the age of atomic bombs is to take measures to guarantee to ourselves in case of attack the possibility of retaliation in kind. The writer in making this statement is not for the moment concerned about who will win the next war in which atomic bombs have been used. Thus far the chief purpose of our military establishment has been to win wars. From now on its chief purpose must be to avert them. It can have almost no other useful purpose.
>
> There are two theories of deterrence, punishment or denial. In principle, a candidate enemy may be deterrable either by the threat to punish him in ways that hurt him very badly or by the threat to defeat his armed forces in the field and thereby deny him achievement of his objectives.

As President Truman struggled with the decision to expand the development of nuclear weapons, U.S. military planners considered their options. Only thirteen bombs existed in the U.S. nuclear arsenal, and some initial U.S. plans were nothing more than carbon copies of the strategies used against Germany and Japan with an atomic twist: existing conventional bombers would drop nuclear weapons on selected cities in the Soviet Union. Other options ignored the nuclear arsenal entirely in favor of conventional bombing attacks against the Communists. In February 1947 the Joint Planning Staff sent the Joint Chiefs of Staff a scenario that assumed the Soviet Union would attack and overrun Western Europe. U.S. planners believed they would not need nuclear bombs to defeat the Soviets if they deployed "a strategic air offensive against vital Soviet industrial installations and war-related facilities in major cities."

This conventional war plan, code-named Pincher, was quickly superseded by Plan Broiler, which for the first time called for the use of nuclear weapons to contain Soviet military advances in Europe while ground forces were built up by the United States. Next came Halfmoon, a conventional strategic air offensive backed up by nuclear weapons. The planners, however, were not certain they could take control of the nuclear weapons in the hands of the Atomic Energy Commission.

President Truman endorsed Plan Halfmoon on 16 September 1948. The policy called on the United States to be ready to "utilize promptly and effectively all appropriate means available, including atomic weapons, in the interest of national security. . . . The decision as to the employment of atomic weapons in the event of war is to be made by the Chief Executive."

Several months later Trojan replaced Halfmoon. The new plan called for a massive buildup of the U.S. nuclear arsenal. It targeted seventy Soviet cities, including Moscow and Leningrad, for bombing by 133 nuclear weapons. A U.S. planning committee nevertheless believed that "the planned atomic attack on seventy Soviet cities would not, per se, bring about capitulation, destroy the roots of communism, or critically weaken the power of the Soviet leadership to dominate the people." The report estimated that "the expected Soviet casualties would be 2.7 million deaths and a reduction in industry of 30–40 percent, but the attack would not halt a Soviet invasion of Western Europe, the Middle East, or the Far East. An atomic attack by itself would not defeat the Soviet Union."

In December 1949 the U.S. government adopted yet another war plan, Offtackle. Unlike Trojan, which targeted Soviet war-making capability, Offtackle was designed destroy the Soviet's ability to wage war and to retard their expansion into Europe. For the first time, U.S. military planners admitted that war with the Soviets was considered almost inevitable.

The United States faced a serious dilemma. The Soviets not only had the bomb but all of Western Europe within easy reach of both their land forces and their current bomber force. Separated by an ocean, the United States had no easy way to deliver nuclear weapons to the heart of the Soviet Union without secure bases in Europe that would be lost with a Soviet invasion of Western Europe. U.S. nuclear weapons of the time were massive (the standard atomic bomb was the aptly named the Fat Man) and required a bomber with an enormous lift capacity and tremendous range. In early 1946 no such bomber yet existed in the arsenal. The solution was the B-36. Bigger than a modern Boeing 747, the B-36 was a giant of an aircraft—indeed, it was the largest bomber ever built.

When the B-36 first hit the drawing board during early World War II, no one imagined it would eventually become the trump card of U.S. nuclear deterrence. In 1940 America was officially neutral, but it seemed only a matter of time before the country would be drawn into the war against Hitler's seemingly unstoppable blitzkrieg. U.S. military planners believed that Britain would succumb to the German juggernaut, and they confronted a strategic vulnerability: no Allied bomber had the range to reach a Europe controlled by Germany. The closest non-European air base was Gander, Newfoundland, over 5,700 miles from Berlin, well beyond the range of any existing bomber.

On 11 April 1941, the Army Air Corps (AAC) issued a daunting challenge for the development of a new long-range intercontinental bomber. Two companies, Consolidated Aircraft Corporation and Boeing Aircraft Company, responded. The specifications stipulated a 275 mph cruising speed, a service ceiling of 45,000 feet, a 10,000-pound bomb payload and a minimum overall range of 10,000 miles. The new super-bomber required a combat radius four times that of the Boeing B-17, the mainstay of the U.S. World War II arsenal.

The new long-range bomber was to be the next in a long line of legendary aircraft, each larger, more sophisticated and more capable than its predecessor. The Boeing B-17 Flying Fortress was the United States' first mass-produced, four-engine heavy bomber. The B-17 had a crew of ten, a maximum speed of 302 mph at 25,000 feet, a range of 3,750 miles and a maximum bomb load of 4,000–6,000 pounds, making it perfect for daylight strategic bombing of German industrial targets. Its successor, the Consolidated B-24 Liberator, served as a heavy bomber in greater numbers than any other bomber in World War II. It also had a crew of ten, a slightly slower speed of 290 mph at 25,000 feet and a shorter range of 2,100 miles, but it could carry a 25 percent larger payload than the B-17. The B-29 Superfortress, one of the largest and most innovative aircraft to see service in the war, was a giant leap forward in design. It boasted a pressurized cabin, a central fire-control

Boeing B-17G during a bombing run. COURTESY USAF

system and remote-controlled machine gun turrets. Though designed as a high-altitude daylight bomber, it gained fame for its low-altitude nighttime incendiary bombing missions over Japan. With its crew of ten, the Superfortress outperformed both its predecessors with a maximum speed of 364 mph at 25,000 feet, a range of 4,200 miles and a maximum bomb load of 20,000 pounds. The B-29 delivered the atomic bomb strikes on both Nagasaki and Hiroshima.

Both Consolidated and Boeing forewarned the Army Air Corps that they were unlikely to meet the specifications for the new intercontinental bomber, especially with the restrictions on human resources and materials caused by the war. Consolidated won the tender on 16 October 1941, largely due to its success in delivering the B-24 Liberator. The company requested a contract of $15 million plus a fixed fee of $800,000 for research and development, mock-up, tooling and production of two experimental bombers initially designated the Model B-35. The first prototype was to be delivered within thirty months and the second six months later. Consolidated extracted a promise that the project would not be "entangled with red tape" and "constantly changing directives." To avoid confusion with the B-35 Northrop Flying Wing, the new aircraft was redesignated the B-36.

Consolidated B-24M in flight. COURTESY USAF

The Japanese warplanes that roared off Japanese carriers on 7 December 1941 and bombed the U.S. fleet in Pearl Harbor drew the United States into the war. Consolidated was instructed to put the B-36 project on hold to concentrate on producing as many of the proven B-24 Liberators as possible. By the end of the war, almost 18,500 Liberators were flying missions around the world.

Boeing B-29 over Mount Fuji. COURTESY USAF

As the war in the Pacific progressed, the newly renamed Army Air Force (AAF) targeted Japan with B-29 Superfortresses from air bases in China. When these bases were threatened by Japanese ground forces, the United States was left without a bomber capable of reaching Japan. Hawaii was the next nearest U.S. air base, and the B-36 was the only bomber in development capable of reaching Japan from there. The AAF ordered Consolidated to ramp up development of the B-36. Consolidated agreed to provide the AAF with a mock-up of the new B-36 no later than 20 July 1942.

Shifting military priorities coupled with design and production challenges repeatedly delayed delivery of the new bomber. Consolidated engineers struggled for over six months to reduce the plane's weight and drag and to eliminate a myriad of other technical problems.

Consolidated modified the B-36's twin tail to a single vertical one, reducing weight by nearly two tons, while decreasing drag and increasing stability. Further changes in the AAF's specifications, however, added more pounds. The recommended Pratt & Whitney engine had been redesigned, adding more than another ton. The army ordered radar and radio systems that required the design of a new antenna system to prevent the plane's weight from increasing another 3,500 pounds. Additional nose guns required an extensive rearrangement of the forward crew compartment. The plane's massive tricycle landing gear assembly did not adequately distribute the B-36's enormous weight on landing, thereby limiting its operation to just three air bases in the entire United States. The army demanded modifications to make landings possible on the same airfields used by the B-29. Convair responded with four-wheel, truck-type landing gear to distribute the load more evenly and even reduced weight by 1,500 pounds.

Despite working round the clock, Consolidated did not have the aircraft ready when the army arrived for its inspection. The 10,000-mile range requirement was proving impossible to meet, forcing reductions in both armament and crew size. The military, facing setbacks in the Pacific, added to Consolidated's problems by refusing to divert scarce resources to the experimental project, which continued to suffer from too few engineers, skilled tradespeople and materials.

By the spring of 1943, China was near collapse, and the B-29 was mired in its own production problems. To strike at the heart of Japan, the United States would need to capture bases in the Japanese-occupied Mariana Islands, located at the outermost limit of the B-29 bomber's range, but the Japanese were not going to give them up without a fight.

In May President Roosevelt and Prime Minister Churchill met at the Trident Conference to focus on the war in the Pacific. They came to the conclusion that "the situation in China was desperate." The Chinese needed a morale boost, and the leaders agreed that the development of the B-36 had to be moved up in the queue of priorities yet again.

In spite of the military's need for the B-36, the order did not include a priority number, meaning that the development of the bomber could be further postponed if the military had more pressing projects. And it did. With victory in the Marianas within the U.S. Marine Corp's grasp, the AAF required more B-29s and its backup, the B-32, also built by Consolidated, which had recently changed its name to Convair. Convair was ordered to delay essential wind tunnel tests on the B-36 until spring 1944 and to stop testing the Lycoming BX liquid-cooled engine in favor of the Pratt & Whitney X Wasp power plant. In the army's opinion, the development of two different engines at the same time wasted scarce resources.

On 19 June 1943, the AAF ordered 100 B-36s at a total cost of $160 million. The first delivery of the much-altered bomber was due in August 1945, the last in October 1946. Both the army and Convair gave themselves wiggle room through escape clauses in the contract. The army was allowed to cut back or cancel the order in the event of excessive production difficulties. Convair would ultimately postpone the delivery dates and increase the cost by $61 million.

In the end the B-36 never saw service in World War II. Just six days after Japan surrendered, Convair finally unveiled the B-36, dubbed the Peacemaker. At its debut before the military brass, the giant bomber couldn't fit through the hangar doors, and Convair had to jack up the nose in order to lower the tail enough to provide clearance. Nevertheless, U.S. military planners were thrilled. They had the long-range bomber

B-36B with its nose jacked up so the 47-foot tail can clear the door. It is also canted sideways so the 230-foot wings can clear the hanger. COURTESY USAF

they now suspected they would need to fight a future war against the Soviet Union. Moreover, the B-36 not only outperformed the B-29 but was half again as cheap to operate in terms of cost per ton per mile.

The giant single wheel on the XB-36 that would be replaced by a truck-type wheel system on production B-36s. COURTESY USAF

On 8 August 1946, almost five years after the Army Air Corps had inked the original order, the B-36 took the air for the first time with test pilot B.A. Erickson at the controls. No one really expected the new aircraft to meet all the requirements posted by the army. No prototype ever did. The specified engines were not yet available, and Convair was forced to use weaker "placeholder" engines for the test flight. Poring over the prototype, AAF inspectors discovered faulty workmanship (caused by a lack of qualified workers), use of substandard materials and deviations from specifications, particularly in the shape of the airfoil. Convair pleaded that the lack of a priority number throughout the war had prevented the company from securing rationed materials. After the war labor woes continued: workers struck at the Fort Worth plant in October 1945 and again in February 1946. The B-36 was grounded again.

XB-36 takes off for the first time 8 August 1946. COURTESY USAF/GD

In 1947 the United States Air Force (USAF) was founded as a service independent of the army and tasked with containing the Soviet Union. Not everyone was happy with the idea of a new and independent air force. Surprisingly, the army generals who lost their air force were not the most offended. It was the admirals of the U.S. Navy who took the greatest umbrage. The admirals, with some justification, believed they had won the war in the Pacific and felt the bulk of an already diminishing defense budget should go to them. When they learned the USAF would have an air fleet more than twice the size of the navy's and only the USAF would have heavy bombers, the admirals went to war in Washington. The B-36 drew the most fire.

Though originally conceived as a way to raise the stakes in World War II, by fortuitous happenstance the B-36 was exactly the right card to strengthen the United States' hand in the growing reality of the Cold War. The B-36's long-distance payload of 10,000 pounds was exactly the weight of the Fat Man atomic bomb, and the aircraft's combat radius allowed the bomb to be delivered from Maine to Leningrad. For the air force, the B-36 could deliver genuine deterrence. For others, the value of the B-36 depended on U.S. resolve to use its nuclear weapons, and that was far from certain with President Truman starting to question the legitimacy of nuclear warfare.

Truman's reluctance caused a dilemma for USAF brass. The doctrine of deterrence relied on the threat of immediate nuclear retaliation. But under the rules of civilian control, the Air Force would need five days to get its twenty-seven specially modified Superfortresses combat ready, secure bombs from an Atomic Energy Commission depot and move the aircraft and bombs overseas to restaging bases. Only then would they would be within range of the Soviet Union.

To provide a credible nuclear threat against the Soviets and to beat back the U.S. Navy admirals, the USAF desperately needed operational B-36s. On 4 December 1947, Convair delivered a plane that was very close to what the production B-36 would ultimately look like. It had a redesigned high-visibility bubble canopy and more powerful and efficient engines. Speeding production up even more, Convair had the first production B-36A ready to fly before the prototype. Score one for the USAF in the battle against the admirals.

XB-36 over Texas. COURTESY USAF

The navy knew that if the B-36 made it to full production, the air force would win the battle within the military that would determine who would patrol the frontline against the Soviets. Describing the B-36 as a "billion-dollar blunder," the navy demanded that the plane's production be halted and that its budget be reassigned to aircraft carrier-based nuclear bombers. In late 1947 the navy presented the Pentagon with plans for the *USS United States*, a super-carrier capable of launching huge fleets of fighter aircraft or nuclear bombers.

First B-36A built by Convair. COURTESY USAF

Countering the navy's maneuvers, the USAF immediately began to train crews on the B-36, using the prototypes available. On 10 April 1948, Captain W.D. Morris and Lieutenant R.E. Munday commanded a night test flight of the B-36 out of Carswell Air Force Base (AFB), successfully dropping its bombs on target from 25,000 feet.

The first production B-36A, named the *City of Forth Worth*, arrived at the 17th Bomb Group at Carswell in June 1948 and was accepted by Colonel Alan D. Clark, 7th Bombardment Wing Commander, and Brigadier General Roger M. Ramey, Eighth Air Force Commander. The bomber's nose plaque proclaimed: "City of Fort Worth First B-36 combat aircraft delivered to Strategic Air Command by Amon G. Carter for the City of Fort Worth where it was built by Consolidated Vultee Aircraft Corporation." Ultimately, the B-36 would be made in a number of modified versions each designated by a letter.

Convair didn't limit its work to engineering and production. The company supported the air force's campaign to win the hearts and minds of the U.S. public by running full-page advertisements in magazines and newspapers across the country.

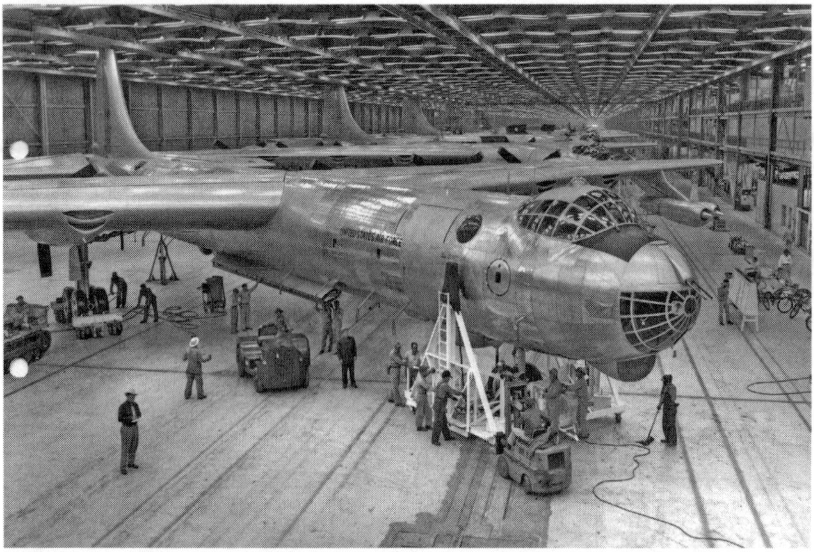

Convair RB-36D, the fourth-generation B-36, on the assembly line at the Convair plant in Fort Worth, Texas. In this iteration jet engine pods had been added. COURTESY USAF

The giant B-36—the biggest land based bomber ever built.

Manned by a crew of 15 men, it is designed to carry 10,000 lbs of bombs 10,000 miles. Its top speed is more than 300 miles per hour. Operating from airports available to us, the B-36 could, [if this country were attacked,] drop bombs on any city in the world.

Just how big is "the world's biggest bomber"?

Imagine a tail fin that is almost as tall as the average 5-storey building! Fuel tanks so large that more than two railroad tank cars are needed to fill them! Six pusher-type engines with a total of 18,000 horsepower! A wingspread as great as that of two B-24 Liberator bombers, with ten feet to spare.

Designed and built by Consolidated Vultee, in conjunction with the United States Army Air Forces, the mammoth B-36 is a mighty symbol of peace-loving America's determination to remain strong in the air—to preserve the peace through strength!

Still looking over its shoulder at the U.S. Navy, the fledgling USAF pressed Convair for more results. While still working to fulfill the order for the first twenty B-36As, the company toiled to develop the B-36B. On 8 July 1948, this new variant made its maiden flight. Its performance surprised everyone, including the USAF and Convair. The bomber maintained an average cruising speed of 303 mph at its combat weight of 227,000 pounds, with a top speed of 381 mph and with a service ceiling of 42,500 feet. For the first time in its long and arduous development, the B-36 not only met but exceeded the original 1941 requirements.

The USAF needed to prove the B-36's long-range threat. On 5 December 1948, a B-36 covered nearly 4,300 miles at an average speed of 303 mph and at an altitude of 40,000 feet. The fourteen-hour flight went off without a hitch. Two days later, on the seventh anniversary of the Japanese bombing of Pearl Harbor, Lieutenant Colonel John Bartlett and his crew lifted off from Carswell AFB. They winged their way toward a special target designed to prove the superiority of air power over naval. Inside the bomb bay of the B-36 was a 10,000-pound dummy bomb and 8,000 miles ahead lay Hawaii. Undetected by the island's naval radar defenses, Bartlett and his crew dropped their bomb directly on target off the coast of Hawaii. Thirty-five and a half hours later they were back in their beds.

The U.S. Navy base commander at Hawaii was apoplectic. Pearl Harbor had been bombed again, and this time by his own country. For the USAF the mission represented absolute victory over the navy and vindication for the B-36. If the giant bomber could reach Hawaii from

Convair B-36A that successfully completed a simulated attack on Hawaii, flying a nonstop round-trip from Fort Worth, Texas. COURTESY USAF

Texas, it could deliver nuclear weapons to the heart of the Soviet Union. Score two for the USAF over the admirals.

The USAF, with one eye still on the admirals and the *USS United States*, took its new super plane on a whirlwind tour. What better chance to show off the potential power of long-range bombers than at the inauguration of President Truman? On 20 January 1949, five B-36s roared over the Capitol building in Washington, D.C. A month later, eleven B-36s participated in an aerial demonstration and static display at Andrews AFB, Maryland, where the president personally inspected the new bombers. Score three for the USAF over the admirals.

B-36 formation flies over the U.S. Capitol, Washington, D.C. COURTESY USAF

The ascendancy of the USAF was almost complete. In the spring of 1949, Louis Johnson— a wealthy lawyer, aspiring politician and a former official of the Convair Corporation—was sworn in as the new Secretary of Defense. He got right to work. The Truman White House ordered military costs cut, and the first victim was the *USS United States*, the navy's treasured nuclear bomber carrier. The cancellation of the giant ship unleashed the famed "Revolt of the Admirals." The opening shot was fired by Cedric Worth, a civilian assistant for "special study and research" to Navy Undersecretary Dan Kimball. Worth produced a nine-page memo for the navy's internal use (though he later admitted giving copies to three members of Congress and to aircraft manufacturer Glenn Martin) condemning the B-36 as "an obsolete and unsuccessful aircraft." Much more damning, the memo charged that the USAF had purchased the B-36 "only after Convair had contributed $6.5 million to various Democratic politicians."

The U.S. Navy publicly accused the USAF of overstating the plane's performance and insisted that it would take twelve hours to get a B-36 ready for flight. The admirals further claimed that the B-36, when airborne, could be shot down by at least three of the U.S. Navy's own fighters. The USAF countered that in simulated attacks against bases in Florida and California the B-36 had eluded frontline navy fighters because its massive wing area allowed it to take evasive action at high altitude, where the fighters had very limited maneuverability.

Outside official political circles in Washington, the Navy League unleashed a broadside of anti-B-36 propaganda. The plane was called "a lumbering cow" and a "billion-dollar blunder" and described as "slow as the old B-24 Liberator" and "far more vulnerable."

By early June the Worth memo was public knowledge. It was leaked by James Van Zandt, a Republican congressman from Pennsylvania and, not incidentally, a captain in the Navy Reserve. Van Zandt demanded an investigation into the "ugly, disturbing reports that the bomber project would have been cancelled a year ago if not for wheeling and dealing by Louis Johnson, other Convair officials and Stuart Symington, the civilian head of the air force."

The air force flyboys struck back, sending Symington to Brookline, Massachusetts, where he gave a speech claiming that the B-36 could "take off from bases on this continent, penetrate enemy defenses, destroy any major urban industrial area in the world, and return non-stop to the point of takeoff." His speech could at best be called wishful thinking, but the public and, more importantly, the media were now believers in the B-36.

In August the U.S. Congress opened hearings into the B-36 affair. The heart of the debate was about not just which branch of the military could best deter the Soviets, but which branch could curry the most favor in Washington. The final blow to the admirals was struck when Cedric Worth testified that he had fabricated the infamous memo on the B-36. "I think I was wrong," he stated. "You made a grave error, did you not?" he was asked. "Yes," was his solemn reply.

The 5 September 1949 edition of *Aviation Week* carried the headline SYMINGTON AND DEFENSE CHIEFS EXONERATED as the House Armed Services Committee gave a clean bill of health to Johnson, Symington, the USAF and Convair. There was not "one iota, not one scintilla, of evidence . . . that would support charges or insinuations that collusion, fraud, corruption, influence, or favoritism played any part whatsoever in the procurement of the B-36 bomber," the committee concluded. The air force's triumph over the navy was complete. The USAF held the cards to the nuclear deterrence strategy against the Soviet Union.

The new bomber shared some similarities with the old B-29 Superfortress. Both had vertical tails. Both had slim, round fuselages. Both had two pressurized crew cabins separated by bomb bays. But their respective sizes differentiated them. Although the Superfortress had been the largest bomber in the U.S. arsenal during World War II, it could comfortably fit under one wing of the giant B-36. The seven-foot-thick roots of the wings of the B-36 had enough room to admit the flight engineers to service the engines and landing gear in flight.

Apart from its sheer size, the B-36 was also distinctive in appearance. A Plexiglas canopy perched forward over the flight deck from which a

Convair XB-36 on the ramp next to battle-tested Boeing B-29 Superfortress.
COURTESY CONVAIR

crew of four flew the plane. A dome below the nose housed a radar antenna. Transparent blisters along the flanks of the fuselage allowed the crew to aim the guns and observe the exterior condition of the aircraft. Six Pratt & Whitney radial piston engines supplied the necessary power. Displacing 4,360 cubic inches each, they were the most powerful and sophisticated piston aircraft engines ever built. The second-generation B-36B carried the R-4360-41 engines with fluid injection. The 500 additional horsepower delivered by the 41s allowed the B-36B to take off from shorter runways and delivered better overall performance. The engines were installed in a pusher configuration (with the propellers facing rearward) to reduce drag, rather than in the tractor style for which they had been designed. Unfortunately, this positioned the carburetors in front of the engine, and in cold and humid weather conditions, ice built up in the carburetor air intakes, increasing the richness of the air-fuel mixture. As many crews were to learn, the unburned fuel in the exhaust caught fire. The B-36 was designed to fly with only three operational engines, but the air force soon learned that the extra stress often caused the remaining engines to fail.

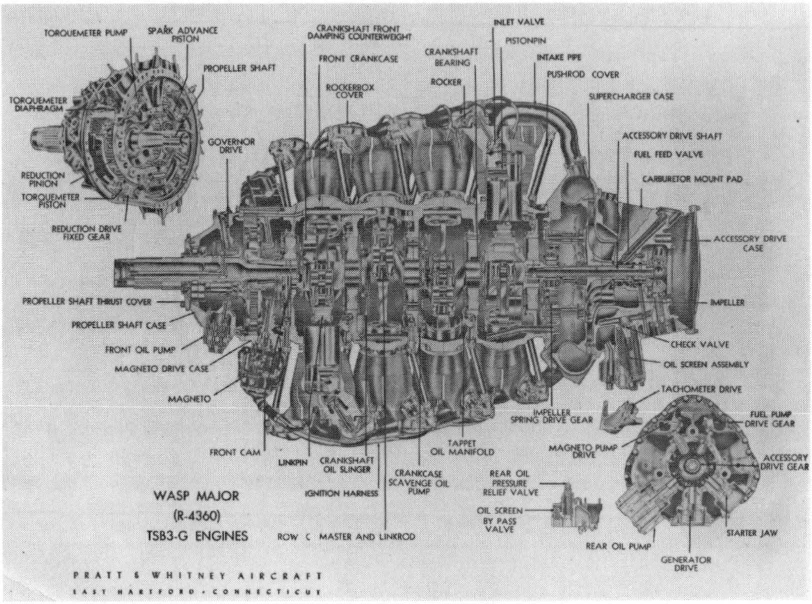

Diagram of the Wasp Major R-4360 engine showing the carburetor mount pad that faced forward. COURTESY PRATT & WHITNEY

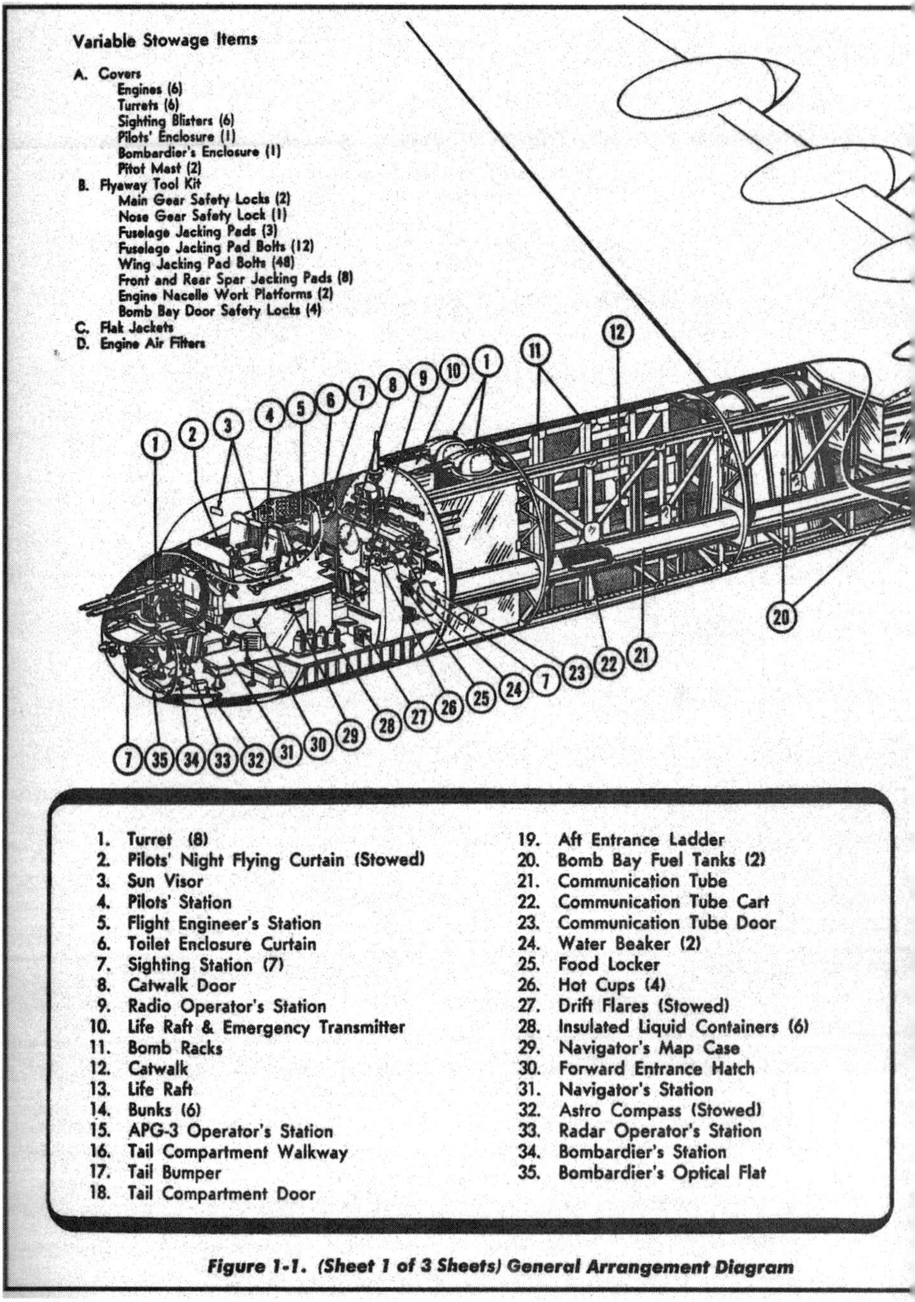

Figure 1-1. (Sheet 1 of 3 Sheets) General Arrangement Diagram

Schematic of the B-36 Peacemaker fuselage showing forward and aft cabins connected by the communication tube running through the four bomb bays.
COURTESY USAF

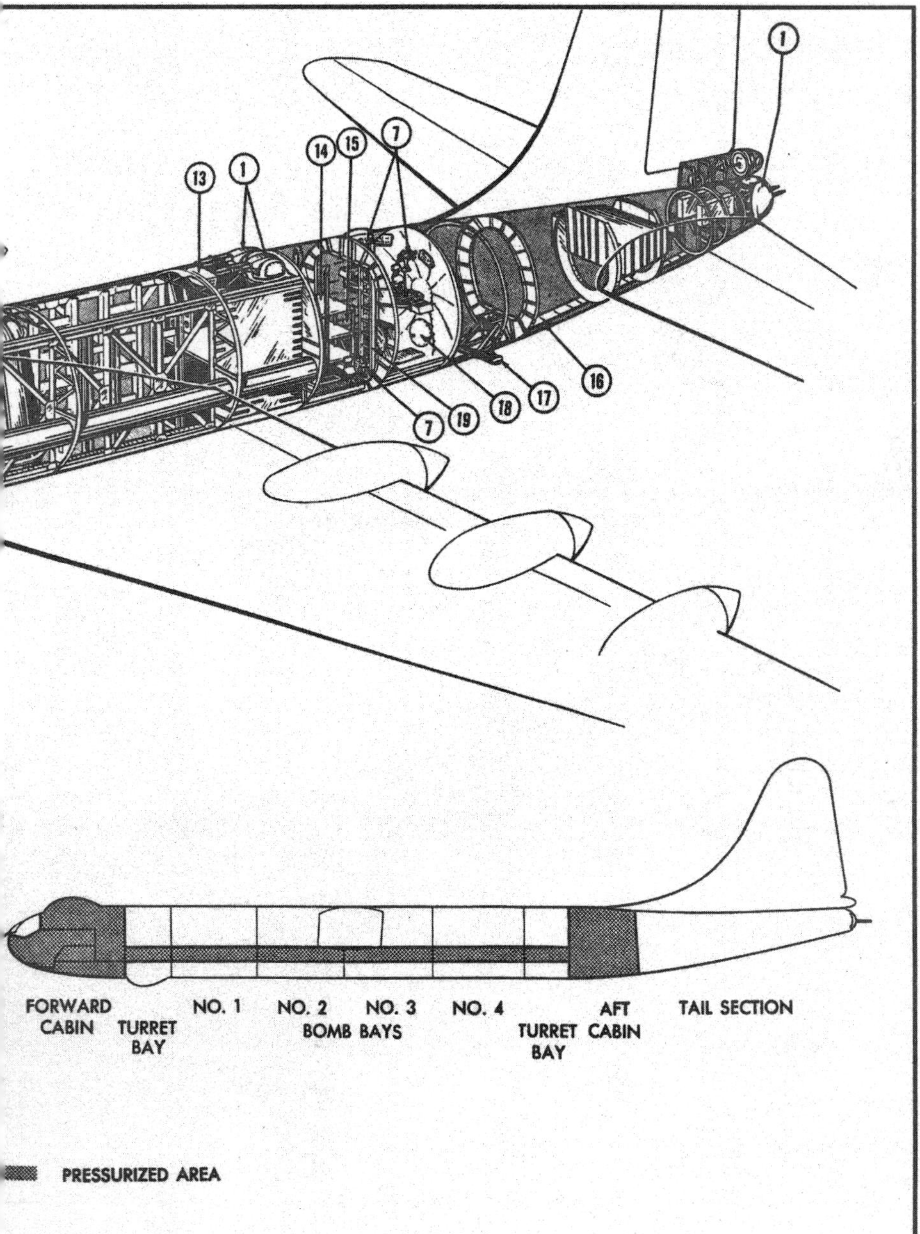

Figure 1-1. (Sheet 2 of 3 Sheets) General Arrangement Diagram

Anyone who heard the roar of the B-36 never forgot it. At 40,000 feet the B-36's six engines rattled windows on the ground. The plane's giant 19-foot propellers, geared to keep the tips from going supersonic, gave it a sound all its own. One observer described it as a "captivating drone. The noise went down to your heels, it was so resonant. . . . You looked up into the sky to try to find this thing, and it was just a tiny cross, it was so high."

The B-36B required a crew of fifteen: a pilot, copilot, radar operator/bombardier, navigator, flight engineer, two radiomen, three forward gunners and five rear gunners. Despite the B-36's enormous size, the pilots and engineers folded themselves into a cramped and uncomfortable cockpit. The engineer faced aft directly behind the

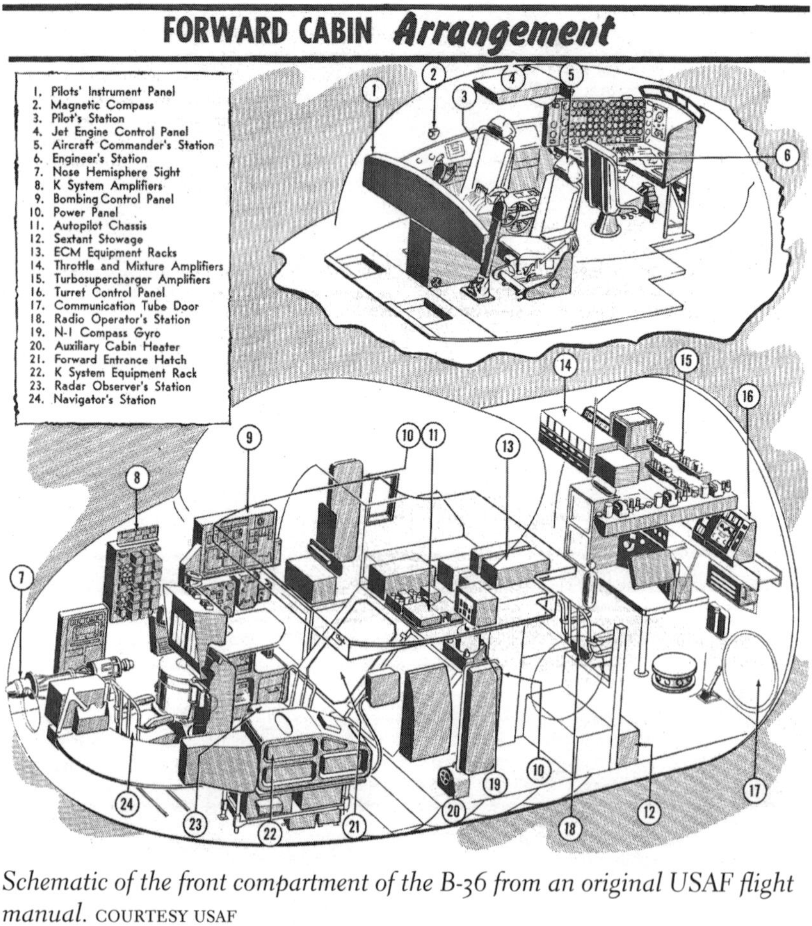

Schematic of the front compartment of the B-36 from an original USAF flight manual. COURTESY USAF

pilots. When the pilots pushed their seats back, the engineer had to move his forward and vice versa. The overhead canopy added to the discomfort. Heat radiating from the large banks of electrical panels kept the interior reasonably comfortable to 25,000 feet, but at higher altitudes the crew had to wear heavy winter clothing, even in summer. Apart from an auxiliary cabin heater, the only other heaters were designed to clear the windows directly in front of the pilots, and the canopy frosted over thickly at high altitude. As the plane descended, the frost thawed and dripped onto the crew on the flight deck.

The ten men in the forward cabin all shared one slow-draining relief tube and a toilet. Both were typically buried under stowed gear, and the tradition developed that the first to use the facilities was responsible for cleaning after the flight. Crew members made sure they lightened their load on the ground before leaving on a mission. Though designed to stay aloft for up to forty hours, the B-36 had only one bunk in the forward compartment, which was normally used to stow extra equipment. No one missed it though as the flight crews generally slept in their seats during missions, preferring to stay near the controls of the massive bomber.

B-36 crewman on the hand-powered trolley in the communications tube that ran between the two pressurized crew compartments. COURTESY USAF

The aft pressurized compartment housed up to five gunners and was equipped with six bunks, an electric range and the world's smallest urinal. The aft compartment also led to the rear gun turret. An 85-foot-long pressurized tube through the bomb bays connected the pressurized flight deck and forward crew compartment with the rear compartment. To travel from one end of the plane to the other, crew members lay on a wheeled dolly and pulled themselves hand-over-hand through the 2-foot diameter tunnel. Few bothered to do so, but they did use the trolley as a dumbwaiter to transport hot meals from the galley in the rear of the plane.

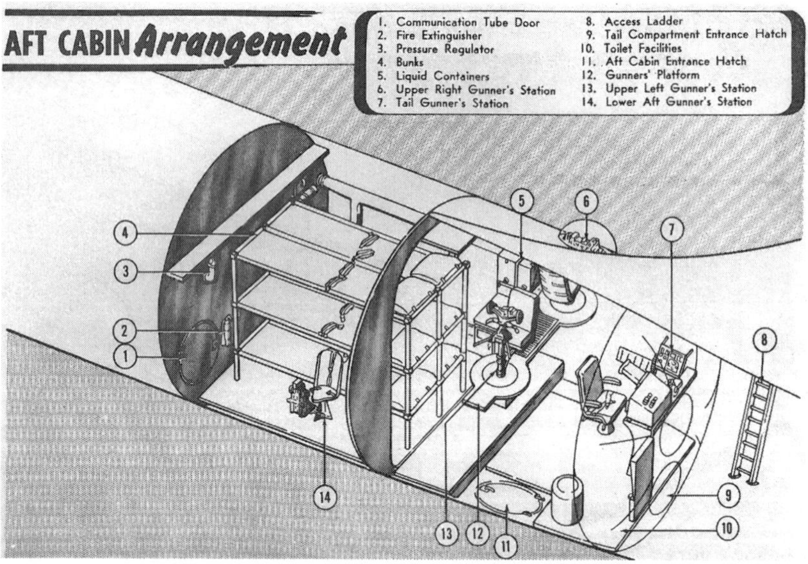

Schematic of the rear compartment of the B-36 from an original USAF flight manual. COURTESY USAF

The B-36B bristled with defensive armaments. The aircraft carried "six remotely operated retractable turrets, each equipped with a pair of 20-mm cannon, plus two more 20-mm cannon in both the nose and tail turrets. This was the most formidable armament ever fitted to any warplane." What made the firepower on the B-36 so devastating was the complex firing system supplied by General Electric. Each of the sighting stations had an electromechanical computer to calculate the target's range and velocity, and the rate of change in its azimuth and elevation. The system was prone to frequent failures, however, because the recoil from the big guns threatened to tear the plane apart.

The B-36 was designed to deliver a massive payload of up to 86,000 pounds of conventional bombs. However, even as Convair was delivering the first series of the bomber, they lacked the details of the still top-secret nuclear weapon. Convair was not alone. At the time even the USAF did not know how many bombs were in the U.S. nuclear arsenal. The B-36 had barely hit the tarmac before it was pressed into service as America's primary delivery platform for the atomic bomb. To perform its new role,

Aft bomb bay of the B-36 showing four 20-mm gun turrets in retracted position at the back. COURTESY CONVAIR AND FRANK KLEINWECHTER

the B-36 was fitted with more and better electronic equipment and special racks in its bomb bays to handle the massive 10,000-pound Fat Man nuclear device.

The bomber's Sperry-built K-1 bombing system ensured an accurate drop of the payload. In its earliest form, the system combined a radar and an optical bombsight with an electromechanical bombing computer. Using the system the bombardier could choose either the radar or optical bombsight to lock on to a recognizable landmark, while the K-1 compensated for crosswinds automatically. With its ability to calculate and compensate, the system also freed the B-36 to take evasive action during its bombing run. During World War II, bombers flying straight and level over their targets presented slow and undeviating targets to enemy fighters and anti-aircraft installations. The B-36's bombing system, coupled with its large wing area, made it practically invincible at high altitude.

For all its size and cutting-edge technology, the B-36 was actually very fragile and prone to frequent failure. According to Jim Little in his *RB-36 Days at Rapid City*, the B-36s were "so flimsily built that the upper wing skin would actually pull loose from the wing ribs. Sometimes you would meet [the plane] with a crew of thirty or forty sheet metal men." As a result, the bomber demanded a heavy maintenance regime.

B-36 with front bomb bay door shown open, sliding up the left side of the bomber, partially covering the numbers. COURTESY USAF

Each of the six engines required a 150-gallon oil tank because the engines burned oil at rates that would be completely unacceptable today. A former ground crewman said, "I don't recall an oil change interval as I think the oil consumption factor handled that." The B-36s often had to return to base early because the engines had sucked the sumps dry of all 150 gallons of oil.

The fifty-six sparkplugs on each of the engines frequently fouled due to the leaded fuel of the 1940s, and mechanics always carried a bucket of extra spark plugs. Maintenance crews had to be constantly vigilant, watching for stainless steel firewalls that cracked, cylinders that overheated and even propellers that reversed in flight or on takeoff.

Outdoor maintenance operations on B-36 at Carswell AFB, 1950.
COURTESY FRANK KLEINWECHTER

Fuel leakage, known as wet-wing, was another of the problems plaguing the B-36. Jim Little wrote that "one airplane leaked so badly the ground underneath was just purple [from dye in the high-octane gasoline]—it was raining fuel under that airplane. The cause—outboard fuel tanks that failed after the wing flexed for a few hundred hours, breaking the sealant."

Outdoor maintenance in winter at Goose Bay, Labrador, Canada. Technicians are rigging heaters needed to warm engines before starting.
COURTESY FRANK KLEINWECHTER

The heavy maintenance regime of the B-36 was complicated by its sheer size. Too large to fit in most hangars, the bomber frequently had to be serviced by maintenance crews working in temperatures as low as –72°F using tools meant for the B-29. The B-36 program was always in a constant state of flux, either subject to reconfiguration or awaiting modification. As a result parts were constantly in short supply. Crews scrounged parts where they could, cannibalizing other B-36s to keep at least some planes operational. Crews were constantly on the prowl for everything from radio tubes to dollies and jacks. In the early years of the B-36 program, a high turnover of ground crews contributed to the plane's maintenance problems.

Plagued with a poor safety record, the B-36 was a death trap if it crashed. To reduce weight the B-36 had been constructed with a high magnesium content. Magnesium, highly flammable, caused the plane to burn rapidly once a fire started. Crews quickly learned not to try to save a B-36. If a crash was imminent, they bailed out.

While recognizing all its design flaws and maintenance issues, many B-36 flight crews acknowledged that the B-36 was a huge advance over its predecessors. Former B-36 pilot Dick Whitfield spoke glowingly of the bomber:

> I loved to fly it. I am absolutely convinced that our having the B-36 during the years it was in service is the one thing most responsible for there being peace and stability in the world today. Given the attitude of the Soviets then and the fact that they knew that we were prepared and willing to respond to any aggressive act on their part was the only thing that prevented them from carrying out their goal of forcibly controlling all of Europe and other parts of the world as well. We can thank the B-36 for preventing this.

Others who flew the B-36 were more ambivalent. Moxie Shirley declared that it "kept the Russians off our backs, but every crew that ever flew that airplane had stories that would make your hair stand on end." Ed Groomsman in *Thundering Peacemaker* called the B-36 "A horrible, lazy beast to fly." Surviving a fiery crash in 1956, he insisted he would rather join the infantry than fly on another B-36.

For all of its scheduling setbacks, production delays, lack of creature comforts and maintenance problems, the B-36 was nevertheless cutting-edge technology. The USAF strategists who assigned tasks to her and the crews who flew her had profound faith in the strategy of deterrence the B-36 was designed to deliver. With a fleet of these bombers, the United States could challenge the Soviet threat of European domination.

The B-36 flight crews were sworn to absolute secrecy about the aircraft, their missions and the payloads they carried. If the top-secret aircraft and its nuclear payload ever fell into Soviet hands, the security of the United States and the free world would be entirely compromised.

If the B-36 was the arrow aimed at the enemy, the nuclear payload the bomber carried was the point. The Mark IV Fat Man was the latest version in a series of ever more deadly atomic weapons that America had begun to develop in 1939 through the Manhattan Project. Eventually, the development of the atomic bomb would employ over 130,000 people and cost a total of nearly $2 billion ($20 billion in today's dollars).

The first atomic bomb, the Little Boy, was 10 feet, 6 inches long, 2 feet, 4 inches in diameter, weighed 8,900 pounds and delivered a force equal to 13,000 tons of TNT. The next generation Fat Man bomb was 7 feet, 8 inches long, 5 feet in diameter and weighed 10,200 pounds—

Replica of Little Boy atomic bomb dropped on Hiroshima, Japan, in World War II. COURTESY USAF

hence its code name. Fat Man became the generic name for a whole generation of early U.S. nuclear weapons. Such weapons had plutonium cores placed in a hollow sphere of high explosive and wrapped in a thin blanket of uranium. When the thirty-two detonators attached to the shell of the bomb were triggered, they crushed the core and unleashed a nuclear explosion.

Nuclear weapon of the Fat Man type detonated over Nagasaki, Japan, in World War II. COURTESY USAF

From 1945 to 1950, the United States produced a small stockpile of Fat Man bombs, all hand-built by engineering specialists in laboratories. However, U.S. military strategists realized that "the bombs were highly idiosyncratic and extremely delicate, not much practical use in the large-scale deployment that was now being envisioned." The military, working with industry, needed to standardize manufacturing and harness the U.S. capacity for mass-production to quickly construct the number of bombs needed to meet the requirements of Plan Offtackle.

Engineers at Los Alamos set to work improving the Fat Man. To correct an aerodynamic wobble that affected accuracy, they streamlined the shape of the case. Early models required a complex arming procedure on the ground, so to improve the speed of deployment, engineers developed a system that allowed weaponeers to insert the core of fissionable material in flight through a trapdoor located in the nose of the casing. Standard operating procedures, however, ruled against transporting the fissionable core and the main sphere containing the high explosives trigger together. Only in time of war, or in a state of high readiness for war, would the nuclear weapon and its core travel together aboard the same bomber. To protect the core in its lead-lined case, engineers developed a special apparatus called a birdcage. The birdcage was equipped with parachutes and a small dingy so that it could be recovered in case of accident.

In the spring of 1948 a series of tests rocked the remote Eniwetok Atoll. The tests proved for the first time that the new nuclear weapons system could be built in a factory setting. All the United States' industrial might in the form of the assembly line would be used to amass the new deterrence arsenal at breakneck speed.

A Special Weapons Command report dated 6 December 1949 concluded that "in-flight insertion gear was operationally suitable for aerial nuclear insertion in all types of atomic bomb-carrying aircraft then in service. No major aircraft modifications were required and no previous training was required for weaponeers." The new iteration of the Fat Man bomb became known as the Mark IV. The weapon could be built in a number of variants from a small one kiloton model to one of twice the power of the version dropped on Nagasaki.

The details of the Mark IV Fat Man remain top secret, as do details of all American nuclear weapons. The United States classified the implosion design of the bomb, and only during the trial of Ethel and Julius Rosenberg in 1951 did some of this information come to light in the courtroom. Photographs of the casings of Little Boy and Fat Man were not released to the public until the 1960s. The original blueprints of the interior of Fat Man are still sealed.

As the United States flexed its industrial muscle to produce the world's largest bombers and most deadly atomic bombs, the U.S. military now needed to mobilize warriors like Theodore Schreier to bring the threat of this weaponry to bear against the Soviet Union. Rushed into production, the B-36's design and maintenance issues would contribute to the harrowing series of events in the early hours of 14 February 1950 when Ship 2075 thundered into the frigid Alaskan winter.

CHAPTER THREE

CURTIS LEMAY AND THE STRATEGIC AIR COMMAND

THE NEW B-36 BOMBER AND THE FAT MAN WERE ONLY THE MATERIALS of the American deterrence policy. To use them effectively, the United States needed highly trained and loyal aircrews to put the bombs on target. Such a force needed a leader who could ignite the men under his command to burn with single-minded determination. If ever a man was born to this destiny, it was General Curtis Emerson LeMay, the firebrand who assumed command of the newly created Strategic Air Command (SAC). As leader he added fuel to the fire and blew on the coals until SAC was a fearsome fighting unit confronting Soviet ambition and a formidable opponent to political rivals inside the U.S. military establishment. An airman's airman, LeMay had been given the challenge of defeating the Japanese during World War II. During the Berlin Airlift in 1947, his transport planes flew round the clock, saving the residents of city from starvation. In the age of nuclear deterrence, he built SAC into the ultimate agent of Cold War brinkmanship.

Curtis LeMay looked liked the guy central casting would send over if a director asked for a pilot. He stood five foot ten, and in his younger years was slim, though he filled out in the fullness of time. Dark-haired with piercing eyes, the general always seemed larger than life, and he commanded every room into which he walked. Even at his wedding, when he married the intelligent and vivacious Helen Maitland, photos captured him with his trademark lit cigar, seeming to freeze him in mid-swagger. It may have been myth, but a story quickly spread through SAC that LeMay had once approached a fully fueled bomber chewing on his lit cigar. When a guard asked him to put it out because it might start a fire, LeMay retorted, "It wouldn't dare."

General Curtis LeMay with his trademark cigar. COURTESY USAF

Often described as brooding, sullen and taciturn, LeMay could share an entire meal with staff without speaking. When he did speak, he sent a barrage of short, clipped sentences that went straight to the heart of the matter, frequently to the point of rudeness. Whatever his faults as a tough, demanding perfectionist, LeMay did not ask anything of his men that he did not ask of himself. He would do anything for his crews, and his men loved him for it.

LeMay was born in Columbus, Ohio, on 15 November 1906 to a typical Midwest family. When he was five, he caught the thrill of aviation. In his autobiography *Mission with LeMay*, he remembered how he chased after the first airplane he ever saw flying high overhead. The die was cast. Curtis Emerson LeMay was going to be a flyer.

LeMay's parents both worked hard to support Curtis and his five younger siblings, though their father changed jobs frequently. LeMay attended Columbus public schools and graduated from Ohio State University with a civil engineering degree. In 1928, still following the dream of flying, he entered the Army Air Corps (AAC) as a flying cadet, and through the Reserve Officers' Training Corps (ROTC), he became an officer. LeMay's dream of the skies was stifled when he learned that his chances of getting to fly on a regular basis were slim in an organization in which officers were considered weekend warriors. In an effort to jump-start his aviation career, LeMay resigned from the ROTC to accept a new commission in the Ohio National Guard. When he graduated from flying school at Kelly Field, Texas, in October 1929, now Second Lieutenant Curtis LeMay resigned his National Guard commission to become a reserve officer in the Air Corps Reserve.

Three months later LeMay received a commission in the regular army. For the AAC during the decade after World War I, airplanes were scarce and flying jobs even scarcer. Most flying-school graduates received their diplomas and were immediately returned to civilian life. LeMay was given the chance to fly, and once he grabbed the control stick, he held on.

LeMay quickly established that he would fly more, work harder and dedicate himself unquestioningly to all things Army Air Corps, an attitude that marked his career to the end. Assigned to the elite 27th Pursuit Squadron of the 1st Pursuit Group located at Selfridge Field,

Michigan, he was soon flying a Douglas 0-2 biplane and logging more hours than any of his colleagues. LeMay also availed himself of all training opportunities, including celestial navigation and instrument flying. Years later LeMay recalled that the chief hazard of all the extra flying time was not the risk of crashing but finding a place to sleep and scrounging enough money to get something to eat. No extra funds were provided for the expenses of either flight or ground crews. LeMay graduated to the army's new P-12 pursuit aircraft, giving him the chance to fly a state-of-the-art fighter. For LeMay, however, fighters were purely defensive, and he believed future air wars would be won on the offensive. He focused instead on the new Martin B-10 bomber, just coming into service, as the way of the future.

P-12 pursuit aircraft. COURTESY USAF

In 1934 President Franklin D. Roosevelt ordered the undermanned and under-equipped Army Air Corps to carry the U.S. mail. Poorly trained pilots flew poorly equipped, obsolete aircraft into night and bad weather conditions. The result: sixty-six accidents and twelve fatalities in the matter of a few months. Before the disastrous airmail program was suspended, the ever-watchful LeMay drew two conclusions that would guide the rest of his career: the overriding importance of logistics and the vital requirement for relentless training. These obsessions helped to earn him a promotion to First Lieutenant in March 1935.

Martin B-10 bomber. COURTESY USAF

Two years later, when the AAC took delivery of the Boeing B-17, the first of a new series of bombers capable of delivering large payloads to distant targets, the new bomber revealed the serious weaknesses in AAC training programs. Most pilots' training had been restricted to following visual landmarks to reach a target only a few miles away. Navigating over long distances at night, or over unfamiliar territory during daylight, required an entirely different set of skills. The AAC needed long-range navigators.

LeMay was reassigned to the 2nd Bombardment Group at General Head Quarters at Langley Field, Virginia. With his uncompromising commitment to excellence, LeMay immediately jumped back into the cockpit, further developing his expertise as a pilot and a navigator. Teaching himself, he soon was also an accomplished bombardier, skilled in using the new and highly classified Norden bombsight. Using his personal experience as a standard, LeMay concluded that airmen trained to perform three different roles would make far more effective and lethal crew members. LeMay began to implement his triple-rated training system. On the ground or in the air, LeMay's men were constantly studying and practicing for war. LeMay's demands earned him the nickname Iron Ass, but he also earned his men's respect. They knew that LeMay's strict training regime would help keep them alive in the event of war.

The army needed to demonstrate the capability of its new B-17 long-range bomber to politicians and the public. They devised a plan to fly

Boeing Y1B-17A in flight near Mount Rainier in 1938. COURTESY USAF

six B-17s to Argentina in February 1938 and three to Columbia in August of the same year. The lead navigator was Curtis LeMay. With no military maps available, LeMay scoured the National Geographic Society for commercial maps and successfully directed the mission. The Argentine flight won LeMay's 2nd Bomb Group the prestigious Mackay Trophy for outstanding aerial achievement. LeMay then pioneered air routes over the South Atlantic to Africa and over the North Atlantic to England, made a solo landing in a Consolidated B-24 and flew the new Liberator to England—all before the start of World War II.

LeMay believed that long-range bombers were America's best hope to win the war in Europe that seemed to be just over the horizon. On 12 May 1938, before the advent of radar, he navigated a flight of three B-17s to intercept the *Rex*, an Italian ocean liner, 776 miles out to sea. The Army Air Corps was thrilled; the navy despaired that even their monopoly of the high seas was being challenged by air power.

LeMay continued to shoot up through the ranks, becoming a captain in 1940 and then a squadron commander in the 34th Bombardment Group. Shortly after, he was promoted to group commander in the Eighth Air Force. Two years later LeMay was a Lieutenant Colonel busy creating and training the 305th Bombardment Group.

Boeing Y1B-17s commanded by Curtis LeMay fly over the Italian liner [Rex] *in the Atlantic.* COURTESY USAF

The 305th continually practiced formation and instrument flying. LeMay himself trained and flew in every position on the B-17 except that of ball gunner. Always searching for ways to drop more bombs on target, LeMay developed a new bombing tactic for the 305th that required his crews to fly long, undeviating bombing runs without maneuvers to avoid enemy fighters and anti-aircraft fire. The tactic was risky and controversial, but the 305th consistently put more bombs on target than other bomber groups. To help compensate for the increased vulnerability of the bombers using his tactic, LeMay developed the combat box, a formation that arranged aircraft in a staggered pattern so all their guns could deliver defensive fire on enemy fighters. LeMay's tactics were adopted by all B-17 bomber units flying in Europe and then by the B-29 Superfortresses in the Pacific.

Even when promoted to Brigadier General, LeMay insisted on personally leading the toughest raids. On 14 October 1943, LeMay, then commander of the Third Air Division, was at the controls of the lead bomber on an attack on the Regensburg, Germany, ball-bearing plant located 500 miles behind enemy lines. Conducted without fighter aircraft for protection, the mission came to be known as Black Thursday for the heavy toll of American servicemen lost. Of the 291 B-17s involved, only 93 returned intact. LeMay defended his actions by saying, "I don't mind being called tough, since I find in this racket it's the tough guys who lead the survivors."

B-17s in formation on a bombing raid over Germany. COURTESY USAF

LeMay's career survived Regensburg. In spite of the heavy losses, the raid destroyed the ball-bearing factory and severely limited Germany's industrial capacity. He was promoted to Major General and became commander of the 20th Bomber Command in India. He then assumed control of the 21st Bomber Command at its Guam headquarters in the Mariana Islands. Still later he became Chief of Staff of the Strategic Air Forces in the Pacific.

In Guam LeMay took possession of the Army Air Force's newest long-range bomber, the B-29. He was not impressed with his aircrews' performance. His bombers were hitting their targets less than five percent of the time and suffered an extremely high rate of attrition. LeMay switched from the high-altitude, precision bombing of Japan to low-altitude, incendiary attacks. He ordered 325 B-29s stripped of gunners, guns and ammunition to allow them to carry more bombs at higher speed. He attacked Japanese civilian populations on the principle that the Japanese war effort relied heavily on cottage industry with families making parts for the military in their homes.

LeMay's B-29s attacked Tokyo just after midnight on 10 March 1945. In a three-hour period, the B-29s, flying under 9,000 feet, filled the night sky, dropping 1,665 tons of incendiary bombs mixed with delayed-fuse high explosive bombs to hamper firefighting efforts. The bombing resulted in the world's first-known firestorm. According to the official Strategic Air Command history:

> The city was a solid sheet of fire, twelve miles across and two miles deep. The heat caused such high winds that bombers in the trailing edge of the formation faced flames 20,000 ft—almost four miles—up. Violent updrafts shot them upward thousands of feet in a few seconds. The firestorm killed more than 100,000 civilians and incinerated sixteen square miles of the city.

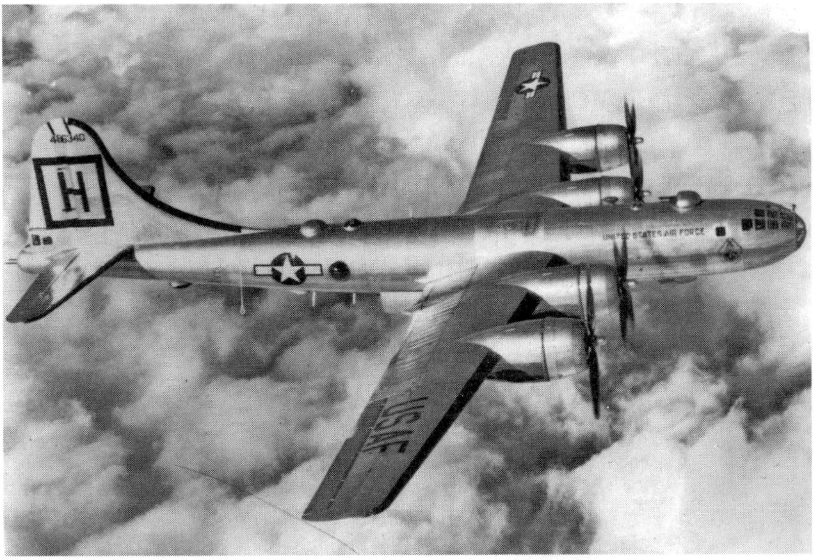

Boeing B-29. COURTESY USAF

LeMay referred to the incendiary attacks on Japanese cities as fire jobs, and he earned the nickname Brutal LeMay among the Japanese. LeMay knew his actions were controversial and once remarked that if the United States lost the war, he fully expected to be tried for war crimes. Speaking of the firebombing attacks in a *New York Times* interview, LeMay stated, "There are no innocent civilians, so it doesn't bother me so much to be killing innocent bystanders. If the war is shortened by a single day the attack will have served its purpose." U.S.

politicians were equally unrepentant. Presidents Roosevelt and Truman supported LeMay's tactics, pointing out that the Japanese had brought the firebombing on themselves by dispersing armament industries into civilian districts.

Cloud of smoke, ash and debris towers 60,000 feet over Nagasaki after the detonation of the Fat Man nuclear bomb.
COURTESY UNITED STATES NATIONAL ARCHIVES

By late summer 1945, LeMay's firebombing tactics had laid waste to almost a hundred Japanese cities. A few cities had been spared—not out of a sense of mercy but so they could be used to test the newest top-secret weapon in the U.S. arsenal. On 6 August 1945, LeMay's 509th Bomb Group dropped the Little Boy nuclear bomb on Hiroshima. Three days later the Fat Man exploded over Nagasaki. The nuclear weapons were the last blows that Japan could absorb, and on 16 August 1945, the Japanese surrendered unconditionally.

Devastation of Nagasaki after the Fat Man nuclear bomb. The partially standing building in the background on the left is the Roman Catholic Cathedral. COURTESY UNITED STATES NATIONAL ARCHIVES

LeMay was convinced that his tactics had won the war. For the first time, an enemy had been forced into submission by a sustained and highly effective aerial bombardment. LeMay was also convinced that nuclear weapons had not been the deciding factor. In his autobiography he insisted that nuclear bombs had accounted for less than one-half of one percent of the bomb damage suffered by Japan; it was conventional bombs that had reduced the country to ashes. In LeMay's mind atomic bombs simply gave the Japanese Emperor the means to save face while surrendering. LeMay marked the end of the war in the Pacific in typical style by piloting a B-29 Superfortress on a nonstop record flight from Japan to Chicago.

With the war over, President Truman struggled determinedly to balance the budget after years of deficit spending. An obvious opportunity to reduce spending was the huge military complex that had been built up to fight the war on two fronts. While it was relatively easy to send hundreds of thousands of soldiers, sailors and airmen home, it was not easy to decommission tens of thousands of fighters and bombers. For one thing, flooding the open market with trainers and transports to be converted to civilian use would devastate the domestic aircraft industry. For another, the latest combat aircraft could not be allowed to fall into the hands of potential enemies. As a result, by June 1946, almost 34,000 decommissioned aircraft had been melted down and recycled into aluminum ingots. In Guam LeMay watched as some of his cherished B-29s were bulldozed over cliffs into the sea.

While the Army Air Force was in the throes of a literal meltdown, LeMay assumed the responsibility for leading the development of new technologies. His new posting took him back to Germany, where he reviewed innovations developed by Nazi researchers and scientists.

Scrapped Boeing B-29s piled up on Tinian Army Air Force Base in 1946. A bulldozer blade can just be seen in the lower right corner of the photo.
COURTESY USAF

Later, when criticized that he put too much emphasis on bombers, he would point out that he had led the investigations into the German V2 rockets. His work in Germany would eventually lead to America's first tactical offensive missiles.

In 1947 the National Security Act created the independent United States Air Force (USAF), and Curtis LeMay, just forty-one years old, was one of its rising stars. He certainly did not complain when the new head of the air force, General Spaatz, ordered him to command the USAF in Europe. LeMay reveled in the opportunity to command again in the field, where he felt he had the most to offer. At his new headquarters at Wiesbaden, Germany, he and his family lived amid the rubble and despair of postwar Germany.

A year later, with less than twenty years of active duty, LeMay was promoted to the rank of Lieutenant General just in time to see the Iron Curtain descend across Europe. Berlin, the former Nazi capital, was now divided among the Allies and isolated deep within Soviet-controlled East Germany. It was no secret the Soviets wanted control

First C-82 used during the Berlin airlift unloading at Templehof Airport.
COURTESY USAF

of the city, and soon they were attempting to starve the allies out. On 24 June 1948, Stalin ordered a halt to freight and passenger trains and water traffic to Berlin. Stalin also cut off electricity to the city, claiming "technical difficulties." The next day General Clay ordered LeMay to dedicate all his C-47s to an airlift to relieve Berlin. Thirty-two flights ferried about 80 tons of milk, flour and medicine. Soon the airlift, nicknamed LeMay's Coal and Feed Company, was growing at breakneck speed as LeMay commandeered C-54s, C-47s and C-82s wherever he could find them.

At Templehof, Berlin's downtown airport, LeMay built a new runway to handle the airlift as it expanded to 1,300 flights carrying an average of 5,000 tons of supplies each day. In late December 1948, Operation Santa Claus flew gifts to the 10,000 children of Berlin. The airlift continued for eleven months, with 213,000 flights bringing in 1.7 million tons of food and fuel. On 11 May 1949, the Soviets conceded and lifted the siege.

LeMay's superiors took note of his success in Berlin. He had proved his ability to combine logistics, planning and especially operations. Washington had found the perfect man to lead the new and struggling Strategic Air Command.

SAC's mission was to:

> be prepared to conduct long-range offensive operations in any part of the world, either independently or in co-operation with land and naval forces; to conduct maximum-range reconnaissance over land or sea, either independently or in co-operation with land and naval forces; to provide combat units capable of intense and sustained combat operations employing the latest and most advanced weapons; to train units and personnel of the maintenance of the Strategic Forces in all parts of the world; to perform such special missions as the Commanding General Army Air Forces may direct.

SAC had its genesis when the United States Army created the Continental Air Forces in 1944 to coordinate four numbered air forces. Soon military planners were recognizing the need for a major command

Strategic Air Command shield, its motto of Peace through Strength pictured in the imagery. COURTESY USAF

devoted exclusively to strategic, long-range air-combat operations. On 21 March 1946, the U.S. Army Air Forces activated three combat commands: the Strategic Air Command, the Tactical Air Command and the Air Defense Command. The Continental Air Forces were redesignated the Strategic Air Command (SAC) and headquartered at Bolling Field near Washington, D.C.

General George C. Kenny, who had commanded the Seventh Air Force in the Pacific, oversaw the creation of SAC, though he didn't actually take command until 15 October 1946. After all the demobilization activity, Kenny only had 148 B-29s under his command, a far cry from the days of the 500-plane raids common during World War II.

By spring 1947 SAC was undergoing a major expansion. Seven new bomb groups were activated at Andrews Field, at least on paper. Lacking enough aircraft and personnel to activate the groups, SAC deployed

B-29s to only two groups. On 16 September 1947, with the United States Army Air Corps re-branded the United States Air Force, army airfields were quickly renamed air force bases (AFBs), and air force personnel were issued new uniforms. The days of army airmen were gone forever. Throughout it all, SAC retained its organization and, more importantly, its mission.

In November 1948 Air Force Secretary Stuart Symington ordered SAC headquarters moved to Offutt Air Force Base in Nebraska, placing the U.S. long-range bomber force well out of the reach of Soviet bombers. By 1949 it was becoming clear that Kenny, a good administrator but not a combat officer, was not the man to lead SAC. Air Force brass turned to General Curtis LeMay to create an effective deterrent to the Soviet threat, and on 19 October 1949, LeMay assumed command of SAC. Air Force Chief of Staff General Hoyt Vandenberg said of LeMay's selection: "[He] has participated in more strategic bombings in time of war than any other man in the world."

When LeMay arrived at Offutt AFB, less than half the available 837 aircraft were operational, and the crews were poorly trained. *Time* magazine reported that soon after his arrival, LeMay found an airman guarding a bomber hangar with a ham sandwich. The story was probably not true but did point to the challenge LeMay had ahead of him. "We didn't have one crew, not one crew, in the entire command who could do a professional job," LeMay wrote of the SAC he inherited.

LeMay's elite Strategic Air Command, with its motto "Peace is Our Profession," became America's pointy end of the stick. It was up to SAC to mobilize nuclear deterrence into such an overwhelming force that the Soviets would not dare attack Western Europe. The first test LeMay set for his new command was a simulated bombing raid on Dayton, Ohio, from 30,000 feet. The only guidance the crews had were photographs taken in 1941, but LeMay reasoned they would have no better than that available for the Soviet Union. LeMay was furious that not a single bomber found its designated target. He responded in his usual forceful fashion: his men would prepare for combat everyday because he believed war could happen any day.

LeMay's superiors recognized in him the unique ability to think analytically but still act operationally. LeMay built his elite fighting force of the very best airman. He demanded for the first time ever in peacetime that crews be on standby twenty-four hours a day. SAC commanders, no matter where they were, had to be available. Wives became accustomed to husbands calling in from movie theaters and restaurants to let headquarters know their location.

Even SAC bases were tested in simulated attacks by security forces to ensure that the organization was always on a war footing. For Ted Schreier and his fellow airmen, there was never a real moment of peace or rest. The security force also ensured that the pilots and their families never forgot that Russian spies always kept SAC bases under close surveillance, no matter where they were located. One story has it that a bomber commander with an ulcer drank up to four bottles of milk a day. When he was scheduled for a six-day mission to Europe, his wife cancelled the milk deliveries. The milkman talked, and people in the community soon remarked that the commander must be on a long mission. A stern reprimand greeted him on his return. The next time he was ordered overseas, the milk deliveries would continue.

LeMay convinced his superiors to allow him the authority to grant spot promotions to aircraft commanders who demonstrated excellence. On the other hand, commanders not meeting his rigorous standards could lose their promotions, often dragging their entire crews down with them.

In spite of his demands upon SAC aircrews, LeMay always put his men first, and they loved him for it. He ensured that his men got pay raises. He wrangled private rooms rather than barracks-style quarters for his crews, and he secured better housing for married men and their families. Together, LeMay and his wife lobbied for better family services. The changes he made were soon adopted across the entire air force.

LeMay's first war plan, conceived in 1949 when America had thirty-three nuclear bombs in its arsenal, was simple in both concept and execution. His bombers would deliver "the entire stockpile of atomic bombs in a single massive attack" on Soviet cities within thirty days. Stalin, unable to counter the U.S. directly, frantically tried to develop a response to the new U.S. strategic bomber force. He ordered huge land armies to be ready to invade Europe if America should attack. The buildup of soldiers and equipment in Soviet-controlled countries in turn provoked the Americans to build more bombers and nuclear bombs. The arms race had begun.

On 29 October 1951, LeMay was promoted to four-star general, the youngest since Ulysses S. Grant. He would lead SAC until June 1957, during which time he would build an all-jet bomber force and lay the plans for America's intercontinental ballistic missile capability. SAC grew to a force of 224,000 active duty personnel equipped with 2,700 aircraft, including 127 B-36s, the mightiest air force the world had ever known. LeMay's reforms proved effective. The reputations of LeMay, SAC and its airmen would become forever linked in the minds of the public. The American public believed in SAC's crucial first line of defense against the Soviets—and the airmen knew it was true. The morale of American airmen had never been higher.

Captain Ted Schreier was thrust into the Cold War. Schreier was an air force officer from Madison, Wisconsin, who had flown many combat missions over Germany during the war. Immediately after being placed on reserve status, he began flying commercial aircraft for the quickly growing American Airlines.

Schreier was older than the average SAC crew member. Born in Cashton, Wisconsin, on 3 October 1915, he was thirty-five in 1950. His

Strategic Air Command B-36 crew. COURTESY USAF AND DON PYEATT

mates averaged twenty-nine years of age, but all had seen combat. Their eyes betrayed their experience: warriors' eyes. These were eyes used to scanning horizons, assessing risks and then taking them. Most were prematurely gray. Nervous exhaustion was common, though none would admit it. Other than his age, Schreier fit the profie of a typical SAC crew member. Having graduated from the University of Wisconsin, he was well educated, physically and mentally fit, resourceful and experienced, patriotic and tight-lipped. He was exactly the kind of experienced combat veteran LeMay coveted. Schreier was called back to active duty. He and his wife, Jean, found themselves temporarily stationed at Carswell AFB outside Fort Worth, Texas.

True to the LeMay philosophy, Schreier had qualified as both a pilot and a navigator before coming to SAC. His superiors recognized his potential and sent him to New Mexico to train as a weaponeer. When Schreier returned from the twelve-week course, he was a qualified atomic bomb weaponeer, an atomic soldier. The job description would change and evolve over time, but not the basic duties. Weaponeers were responsible for anything and everything involving the nuclear weapons in their charge. Schreier's job was to provide and test certain bomb components, and to supervise and inspect the Fat Man's assembly. He tested completed units. He coordinated overall weapons-related project activities and responsibilities for missions. He certified the satisfactoriness of the devices. He oversaw all bomb-handling duties prior to takeoff, including loading the bomb aboard the aircraft. He provided advice and recommendations pertaining to the atomic bomb's use. The Fat Man was complicated technology. By the time Schreier was made a weaponeer, the bomb, in its fourth iteration and now dubbed the Mark IV, was the world's most deadly weapon. Besides its plutonium core, the bomb contained 264 pounds of uranium and 5,300 pounds of high explosives in its shell.

Schreier and his crewmates trained each and every day. Each cycle of training served up endless variations on a routine: twelve to sixteen hours in the air, more hours in preflight briefings and postflight debriefings. SAC flights left the continental United States around the clock, simulating bombing missions on the Soviet Union. Shoehorned into tiny cockpits and flight decks, the crews knew the drill. A B-36 on a training run would head out on an average twenty-hour mission, then would loop back and set its bearings for an American city that resembled an enemy target with the goal of simulating the dropping of an atomic bomb on target. They had to avoid detection by ground radar or by fighter interceptors that had been alerted to an imminent raid. The window-rattling drone of the B-36 was a lullaby; citizens could sleep soundly knowing that SAC was overhead. Lieutenant General James Edmundson, one of LeMay's deputies, remembers feeling that he was on "the cutting edge of the Cold War. . . . If we slipped, if we were not capable of doing our job, then the Russians would eventually move in and take over. We didn't know [whether] they'd come and outright bomb us, but there were other things that they might do that would trigger machinery in Washington which would launch SAC. . . . It was a tough life."

No doubt Ted Schreier shared these sentiments. As he prepared to supervise the loading of the Fat Man into the bomb bay of a B-36, as he checked the detonating charges, as he secured the birdcage inside the fuselage, whether armed with a nuclear core or a lead training dummy, Schreier must have experienced both trepidation and resolve. And he wouldn't have exchanged his experience for anything in the world.

Early Carswell Air Force Base gate sign showing the B-36 Peacemaker.
COURTESY FRANK KLEINWECHTER

CHAPTER FOUR

The Flight of Ship 2075

When Captain Ted Schreier and his fellow crew members in Ship 2075 flew from Alaska in February 1950, their mission was the latest in a series of ever more elaborate tests of Strategic Air Command readiness and execution. In the preceding years, SAC, under the command of the ever-vigilant General LeMay, trained for long-range missions to the far corners of the earth by flying the B-29 on simulated bombing runs on U.S. cities. Called "maximum-effort" missions, the flights tested both aircraft and crews under near-combat conditions, including evading detection and interception. In 1947 simulated raids were flown on Los Angeles in April, New York in May and Chicago in August. Maximum effort was an appropriate name: the mission against New York alone involved 101 B-29s. "People were down there in their beds," LeMay wrote in his autobiography, "and they didn't know what was going on upstairs. San Francisco had been bombed over 600 times in a month."

By 1948, even as kinks in design and production were still being smoothed out on the giant new B-36 bomber, the air force commenced flight training. On 14 May 1948, Captain Wesley D. Morris and First Lieutenant Richard Munday took part in a thirty-six hour flight that covered over 8,050 miles. They successfully dropped thirty-one bombs from 25,000 feet on target at night using radar. Only four days later, Captain Morris again crewed on a B-36 training run, this time as a bombardier, true to LeMay's concept of triple-trained personnel. From 31,000 feet he dropped twenty-five bombs on the Naval Range at Corpus Christi, Texas. In August of the same year, a B-36A flew an endurance test of 5,500 miles over twenty-six hours, using 14,000 gallons of fuel. In

January 1949, a B-36B piloted by Major Stephen Dillon dropped two dummy Grand Slam bombs on target, one from 35,000 feet and one from 40,000 feet. The crews were thrilled with the B-36, and training continually produced new records and successful results.

Ship 2065, Ship 2075's closest sister, readied for takeoff. COURTESY USAF

In March 1949 the B-36 began the first of many extensive combat-type training missions inside the United States to test its ability to evade detection and interception. A B-36 flew a modified training regimen that lasted over forty-four hours. The bomber left Carswell Air Force Base, Texas, flew north to Minneapolis, Minnesota, turned west to Great

B-36A over Carswell Air Force Base, Fort Worth, Texas. COURTESY USAF

Falls, Montana, then south to Key West, Florida. It dropped nearly 10,000 pounds of bombs over the Gulf of Mexico before flying over Houston. From Houston the B-36 flew back to Fort Worth, Texas, then north to Denver, Colorado, and on to Great Falls, Montana, before turning west to Spokane, Washington. On the last leg of the flight, the bomber developed engine trouble over Denver and was forced to return to Carswell. The flight was the longest recorded to date in a B-36.

Having proven the B-36's endurance, though not its reliability, SAC turned its attention to Alaska the next year. If B-36s could operate out of Alaska, they would be within range of virtually any target within the Soviet Union. Military planners selected the base at Fairbanks, which had been constructed during the war, as the ideal site for a B-36 bomber base. Strategic bombers needed a much longer runway than those constructed during World War II, so the military ordered the west runway lengthened to 14,500 feet. By November 1947, the 97th Bomber Group was on station in Alaska, flying B-29 bombers from the newly renamed Eielson Air Force Base (in honor of famed Arctic aviation pioneer Carl Ben Eielson).

The harsh Alaskan winter immediately presented a formidable obstacle to aircrews flying in and out of Eielson. Rapid temperature swings, severe thunderstorms with hail and lightning, snow in summer and bolt-snapping winters lasting from late September to mid-April were typical:

> [Winters] are very cold and dry, with temperatures sometimes dipping down to –60°F. Usually the temperature is below zero [Fahrenheit], almost for entire months. The coldest temperature ever recorded in Fairbanks was –66°F on January 14, 1934. The average January low is –19°F and the average January high is –2°F. . . . During the winter months, if the temperature drops below –20°F, ice fog can occur. On Dec 21 the sun is only up for 3 hours and 42 minutes with 6 hours and 33 minutes of usable daylight.

On 25 July 1949, Major General Roger M. Ramey, Eighth Air Force Commander, and Colonel William Fisher, 7th Bomb Wing Commander, flew two B-36s to examine the facilities at Eielson. The base passed the

B-36s on the ground during winter training exercises. COURTESY USAF

test. In September of that year, the 7th Bomb Wing was instructed to establish a forward operational area for future training flights to Alaska. Code-named Operation Drizzle, the plan was to test both the facilities at Eielson and the cold-weather capability of the B-36. In September a Special Weapons Unit left Sandia, New Mexico, for Eielson. The unit ran a limited assembly exercise and prepared for a second test later in the winter. According to all reports, the September exercise was completed without problems.

LeMay concluded that the extreme Alaskan climate posed too many risks for the giant B-36 and ordered the field to be used only as a staging point from which bombers would return to their home bases in the continental United States. Crews called these training missions "flying around the flag pole." According the LeMay's plan, in the event of war, combat crews would be ferried to Eielson to await the arrival of their B-36s flown in by shuttle crews. The combat crew would then take off from Alaska, bomb their Russian targets and land at bases in Europe or the Middle East.

Line of parked B-36s during winter at Goose Bay, Labrador, Canada.
COURTESY FRANK KLEINWECHTER

The ink was hardly dry on the order to establish a B-36 bomber presence at Eielson when military planners began devising the first full-scale practice of an all-out nuclear strike against the Soviet Union for the following February. According to Major Taylor of the 7th Bomb Wing,

> [our] original plan was to take off from Eielson and the strike aircraft were to return . . . to Carswell Base via various routes throughout the United States. On the flight back we were flying a complete profile of our simulated combat missions . . . to ensure our tactical readiness, our ability to go out and perform a combat mission. . . . The general principal behind the maneuver was to fly to Eielson, refuel, change our ferry crew, put our combat crew on at that point and fly to any part of the world that the Strategic Air Command may direct, and land at some other base or return [to Carswell].

An important component of the proposed training mission pitted the operational capability of the B-36 against the harsh Alaskan climate. As with most bases, Eielson's hangars could not accommodate the B-36's enormous size, and the ground crew would be required to repair, outfit and arm the B-36s without shutting down the engines, which would quickly freeze solid in the frigid temperatures. One of the B-36s chosen for the cold-weather mission, Ship B-36B 44-92075, commanded by Captain Harold L. Barry, would carry a nuclear weapon, the 10,000-pound Mark IV Fat Man. General LeMay had managed to wrest the atomic bomb from the Atomic Energy Commission, which would ferry the device to Eielson from one of its four nuclear weapons storage sites. The mission's pilot, First Lieutenant R.P. Whitfield, explained the importance of training with the real thing: "Without a real bomb the support systems could not be tested. . . . This mission was to be as real as it gets short of war." Barry's mission briefing called for the flight to skirt the coast of British Columbia, Canada, simulate a bombing run on San Francisco, California, and return to base in Texas without being detected by defense forces stationed along the way.

The air force was anxious for the secret mission to succeed without incident. George Chadwell, Group S-4 (Squadron Operations Officer) of the 7th Bomb Group, was in Eielson for the operation. He recounted

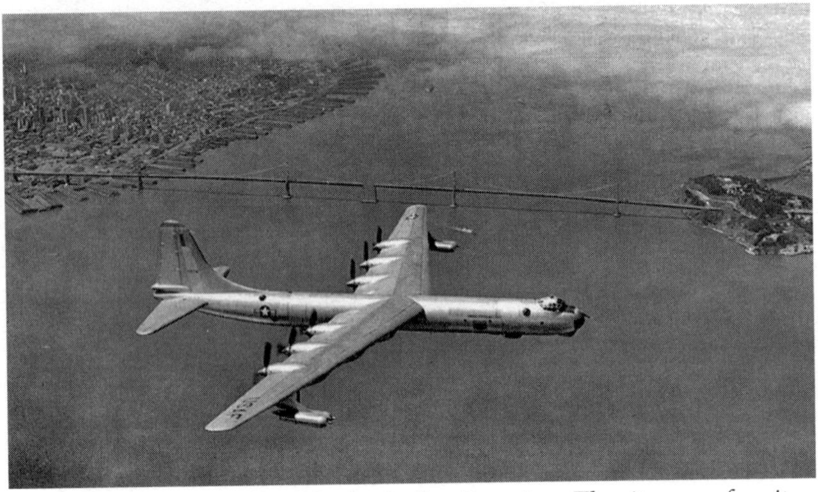

B-36 flying over the Oakland Bridge in San Francisco. The city was a favorite practice target for General LeMay's Strategic Air Command. COURTESY USAF

the preparations: "The formal briefing for the combat crews on B-36 AF Number 44-92075 [Barry's mission] was conducted at Carswell AFB, 1 February 1950. Specialized briefings were conducted after the formal briefing for pilots, observers, flight engineers, radio operator and gunners." Colonel Blanchard, Director of Operations, Eighth Air Force, further explained that "the briefing covered communications, their routes, the target, and duties of each and every one of the members of the crew."

On 2 February 1950, Barry and his crew boarded a C-54 Skymaster at Carswell AFB for the flight to Eielson. The crew members included:

- Airplane Commander: Captain Harold L. Barry

436th Bomb Squadron target study class.
COURTESY USAF AND FRANK KLEINWECHTER

- First Pilot: First Lieutenant R.P. Whitfield (also a B-36 airplane commander in the 436th Bomb Squadron)
- Copilot and Weaponeer: Captain Ted Schreier
- Navigator: Captain William (Bill) M. Phillips
- Radar Operator and Navigator: Lieutenant Paul Gerhart
- First Flight Engineer: Lieutenant Ernest Cox
- Second Flight Engineer: Lieutenant Ray Darrah
- Third Flight Engineer: Lieutenant Charles Pooler
- Bombardier: Lieutenant Holiel Ascol
- Gunners: Staff Sergeants Neil Straley, Elbert Pollard and Dick Thrasher; and Sergeant Martin Stephens
- Radio Operators: Staff Sergeant Jim Ford and Sergeant Vitale Trippodi
- Radar Mechanic: Corporal Richard Schuler
- Observer: Lieutenant Colonel Daniel MacDonald

SAC handpicked the crew for this maximum-effort mission for their expertise, experience and loyalty. SAC was determined nothing would go wrong on this first crucial training flight with a nuclear weapon aboard. In a deviation from standard procedure, Lieutenant Colonel MacDonald joined the crew as an observer. While the U.S. Air Force

U.S. Air Force C-54 of the type used to ferry the mission crew of Ship 2075 to Alaska. COURTESY USAF

has never revealed the Colonel's official role, it is widely believed he was there to baby-sit the atomic bomb as another level of insurance for SAC and the Atomic Energy Commission. In another deviation from standard procedure, Ship 2075 had two copilots. SAC usually assigned crews to the same aircraft for all missions. However, for the February mission, SAC selected the bomber normally piloted by First Lieutenant Whitfield. Whitfield was offered the choice between staying behind or acting as copilot to Barry. Whitfield took the busman's holiday. Typical of SAC pilots, he went along to look after his aircraft.

The crew of Ship 2075 reached Eielson on 3 February 1950, the day their top-secret mission was scheduled to begin. At the base, temperatures plummeted to as low as –51°F, and the mission had to be delayed because refueling units froze at temperatures lower than –35°F. The cold snap lasted for days. Barry and his crew used the time to rest and prepare.

Ten days later the mercury edged up to –27°F, and the mission was ordered to proceed. Colonel Bartlett and his crew ferried Ship 2075 to Eielson from Carswell AFB. He reported that "all was well with the pre-flight check" and that it was "in all, a very fine trip up."

In spite of Bartlett's claims, a number of technical problems plagued the flight to Eielson. Before landing, Bartlett noted a slight creeping of the number four propeller that the flight engineer diagnosed as an oil shortage. Following regulations, Bartlett described the engine problem when requesting final permission to land. The tower needed to determine whether the problem could be repaired at the base. If not, the flight could be waved off and ordered to return to Carswell. After deliberating, the tower gave permission for Bartlett to land. As he settled the huge B-36B down onto the windswept runway, the temperature was –40°F. He taxied the giant bomber to the refueling point and left the engines running as instructed. He then reported other critical problems to the ground crew: a hole in the water tank for the turbo on engine number five and an inoperative fuel-tank boost pump on the number two bomb bay fuel tank.

Following standard procedure, the ferry crew loaded their gear onto a truck, including Ship 2075's Aldis Lamps that were critical for the crew to observe the exterior condition of the B-36 during night flights. The lamps were in short supply and were not to be removed from the planes, but, as usual, the ferry crew was scavenging for their next flight. The truck headed back to the crew quarters, and Bartlett's team headed to their debriefing. After the debriefing, the second engineer returned to Ship 2075 to start the refueling process. He would be the last of the ferry crew to see his bunk at the end of a very long day.

All of Commander Barry's crew had bedded down early the night before the mission, knowing the importance of the flight ahead of them. Colonel Chadwell recalled that the officers left the Officers' Club early and that he told them he would see them at the morning briefing. At 8:30 AM on the morning of 13 February 1950, Commander Barry and his crew tramped through the frosty dark of the Alaskan morning to the nondescript briefing room at Eielson.

Barry's crew made final preparations for the mission ahead. They knew from the earlier briefings that their training flight simulated the profile of an actual combat mission, including night and high-altitude flying. From Anchorage, Ship 2075 was to fly to Cape Flattery (at the entrance to the Strait of Juan de Fuca) at 14,000 feet before climbing to 40,000 feet and continuing to Fort Peck, Montana. There it would bear south to the Gulf of California. Then Ship 2075 was to turn toward to the Pacific coast and fly north to test the California coastal radar defenses before making its simulated bombing run on San Francisco. Finally, the bomber would head east to return home to Carswell AFB in Texas. The twenty-hour flight plan was designed not to enter Canadian airspace which, in the 1950s, extended only 12 miles off shore.

The mandatory preflight briefing was the last chance for senior officers to judge the readiness of the crew for their mission. It was also the last opportunity for the brass to make any changes to the mission profile. Colonel Roberts, the Task Force Commander at Eielson, did not attend the briefing, sending Colonel Chadwell instead. The orders to the crew were subject to interpretation. "Despite icing conditions," Roberts later testified, "the instructions given to Barry and his crew [were] that they were to fly the mission as planned in the profile, but to avoid the icing conditions which were forecast." Barry and his two co-pilots, however, were convinced in no uncertain terms that only if the bomber was in real danger were they to deviate from their assignment. The flight plan would leave Ship 2075 with a 3,000-gallon reserve when it landed at Fort Worth, Texas. However, this calculation was valid only if the bomber maintained the lower altitudes planned for the early part of the mission. If forced to fly at higher altitudes, Ship 2075 would not have enough reserve fuel to both complete the mission and touch down safely back at Carswell AFB.

Colonel Chadwell later reported that he personally completed the briefings for the flight engineers and airplane commanders, while Major McWilliams gave the briefings for the observers. Lieutenant Jones provided the weather briefing, which called for clear skies, temperatures of –26°F, severe icing up to 10,000 feet, rime icing above 15,000 feet and "not much" icing at 17,000–18,000 feet.

The crew then reported to Colonel Flikenger, Eighth Air Force Flight Surgeon, for a full preflight physical. Flikenger found no evidence of illness or fatigue, and all crew members received approval to fly. The crew of Ship 2075 were cleared for takeoff for a test of weapon systems with a nuclear bomb aboard. While the official records now admit to the bomb's presence, the air force has always denied that the plutonium core was aboard. About the size of a softball, the core contained the nuclear fuel necessary for the implosion-type device. The air force's claim is consistent with the memory of copilot Whitfield, who recalled that the bomb core on board was a dummy made of lead. Nevertheless, the Fat Man aboard Ship 2075 contained a uranium shell and conventional explosives that made it a live dirty bomb capable of dispersing considerable radiation. Also on board was the birdcage bolted to the wall in the same bomb bay as the bomb. The birdcage weighed about 90 pounds and had a lead-lined container in which the bomb's plutonium core (or the lead dummy) was stored. The new Mark IV Fat Man allowed the weaponeer to transfer the core to the bomb while in flight, but Whitfield later reported that, "the mechanical systems for handling the core were not installed for this flight."

As weaponeer, Captain Schreier personally supervised the loading of the bomb. In the feeble light of the frigid sub-arctic day, a crew pulled a curtain around the open door of bomb bay number one to ensure that no prying eyes could witness what they were hoisting into the B-36's bomb bay. As the bomb was lifted into the specially designed racks, Schreier clambered into the plane to double-check that the bomb was securely locked in place. He then ordered the bomb bay door closed and secured.

Like any complicated aircraft, the B-36 required many hours of ground maintenance for each hour in the air. Typically, a skilled ground crew took six hours to prepare a B-36 for a mission. The ground crew, working outdoors in frigid temperatures on Ship 2075, had just three hours of natural light to load the bomb and complete all required maintenance. After the ground crew completed their work, the flight crew usually needed another hour for the preflight check involving six hundred separate steps.

The ground crew scrambled to address the maintenance issues in the finger-numbing cold. In describing the maintenance performed on Ship 2075 that morning, Colonel Roberts reported that repairs were completed on the number two bomb bay boost pump, the number four propeller, and engines three and four. However, he also reported that time ran short to fix other problems. The unfinished repairs included the hole in the number five engine water tank, the jammed radar tilt antenna, the broken number two bomb bay cables (the doors could be closed but not opened) and the manifold pressure transmitter and turbo on engine number six. In spite of the remaining problems, Roberts reported that "the airplane was in good condition—all of these [problems] were minor."

Commander Barry's crew hurried through the process of loading personal and mission gear aboard the B-36, including winter survival gear, parachutes, spare parts lockers, drinking water and in-flight meals. The official manifest recorded the loading of twenty-two parachutes, twenty vest-type life preservers, twenty pneumatic one-man rafts, twenty anti-exposure suits, five survival kits and five Arctic and mountainous terrain supplements. Formerly, standard equipment included six-person survival rafts, but SAC had just issued a new directive that, in event of serious trouble over water, crew were to bail out and send their aircraft out to sea on autopilot rather than try to ride their planes down and ditch in the water. Finally, an emergency radio, known as a Gibson Girl, was thrown aboard. The Gibson Girl was used by crews to broadcast their position if forced to abandon the aircraft. Using direction-finding equipment, a rescue party could take bearings from the distress signals to determine the crew's location or follow the signal to its origin.

As provisioning of the plane continued, Barry, Whitfield and Schreier (back from supervising the loading of the bomb), as well as the navigator, bombardier and co-observer, collected the final mission and weather information. The engineers put pencil to paper, scratching out the calculations for nose-up takeoff and flaps-up speeds, which depended on aircraft weight and temperatures. They performed all weight and balance checks, planned mission fuel loads and calculated engine power settings for all legs of the flight. The engineers' preflight checks also involved "crawling the wing." While Cox did the paperwork, Second Flight Engineer Lieutenant Ray Darrah crawled into the wings to do the mandatory checks. He clambered up the left main landing gear into the wing to check fuel and oil lines and numerous fuse and circuit breaker panels. Then he completed the same procedure on the right wing. Despite the freezing temperature, Darrah emerged soaked with sweat from his exertions.

The ground crew tinkered with last-minute maintenance even as the flight crew ran through their preflight checks. Tempers frayed as

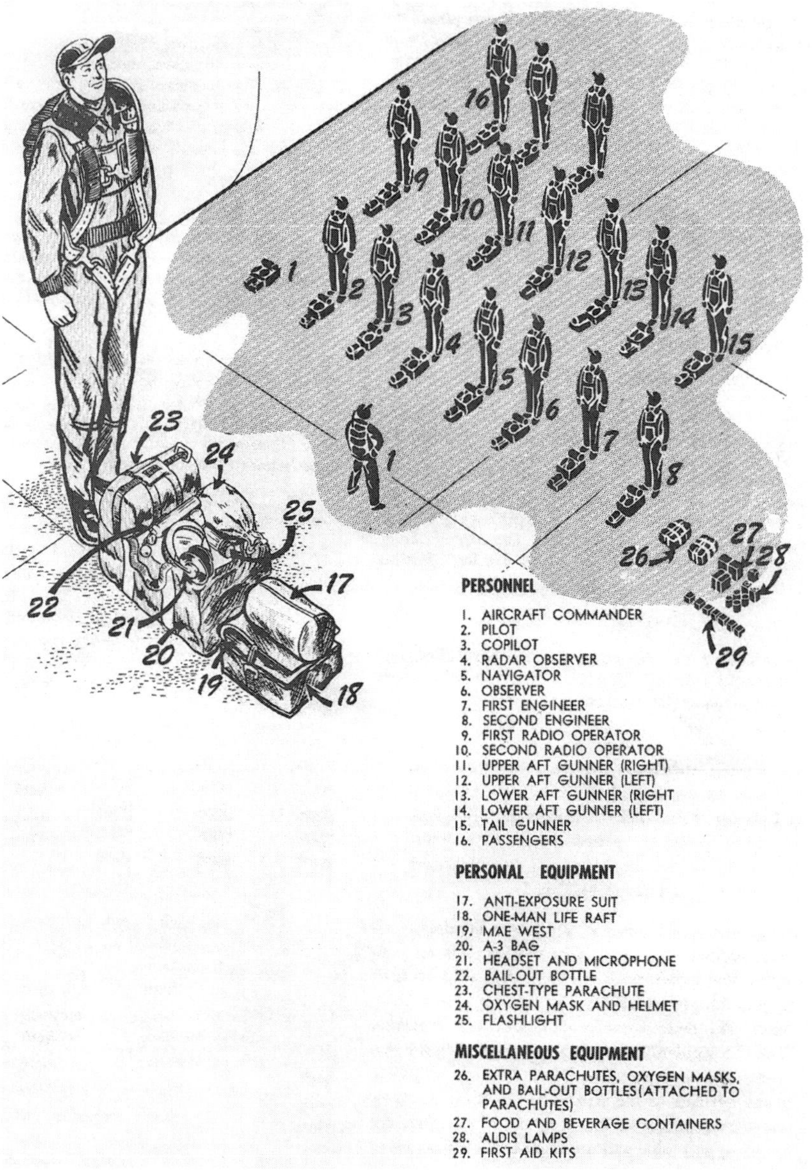

Personnel and personal equipment on the B-36. COURTESY USAF

takeoff time approached and the window for takeoff was closing as the winter dusk approached. Fuel samples were sent for testing out of concern that it might contain water due to condensation at the freezing temperatures. The ground crew put pressure on the testers to return the

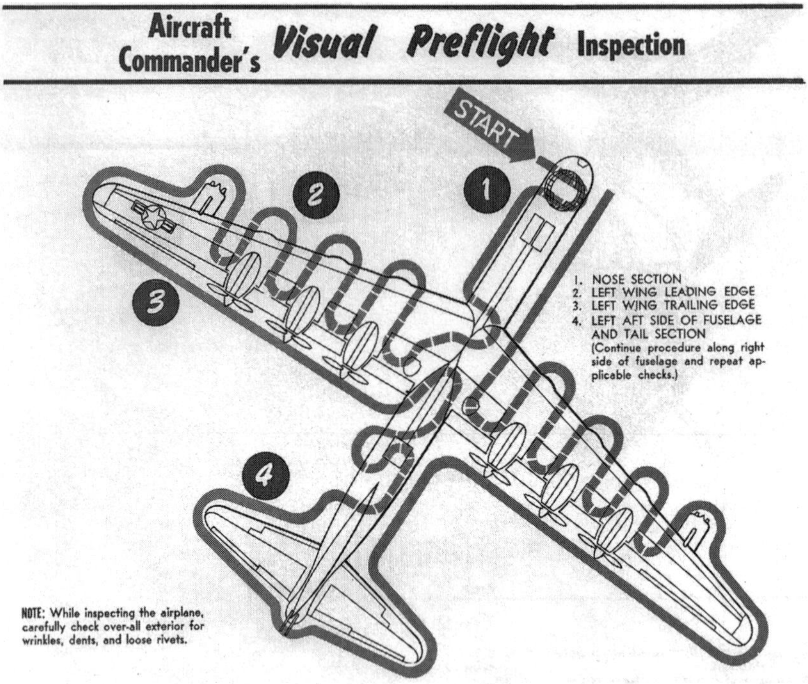

Aircraft commanders' visual preflight inspection instructions. COURTESY USAF

results quickly. The word came back that the fuel was approved to load. First Flight Engineer Cox recalled that the B-36 was loaded with 18,000 gallons of fuel in the wings in addition to the 3,000 gallons of fuel in the number three bomb bay tank and 2,400 pounds in the number two tank. Captain Baulch, Engineering Officer at Eielson, reported that the "refueling units had been in the hangar thirty-six hours and the temperature of the hangar was approximately 32°F." Investigation later uncovered that the samples had been taken incorrectly and that the fuel might indeed have been contaminated with water.

After completing their preflight activities, Barry and his aircrew lined up for a final inspection of both emergency and personal gear before boarding the aircraft. While the crew boarded and took their assigned positions, Barry personally undertook a visual inspection of the giant bomber. Fretting about the list of uncorrected mechanical deficiencies, he walked around the giant B-36. The six engines thrummed at idle as the winter wind whipped over the airfield. Slowly,

Crew positions for takeoff and landing in the B-36. COURTESY USAF

he made his way to the entry gangway and hoisted himself in. Later he would recall his misgivings about the speed with which the B-36 had to be turned around by the ground crew.

Cox, wedged in front of the three-section panel of instruments behind the pilot, went through his engine run procedure. Dick Thrasher, the gunner and scanner, crouched outside to watch for engine trouble, communicating with Barry and Cox through the B-36's interphone. Thrasher then worked through his checklist, ensuring that safety locks and protective covers were removed, armament doors were closed and static ground wires were disconnected. He gave the all-clear and clambered aboard.

Commander Barry called for the crew to assume takeoff positions. With Barry, Whitfield, Cox and Darrah in their assigned seats, the rest of the crew in the forward cabin—Schreier, Phillips, Gerhart, Pooler, Ascol and MacDonald—crammed themselves on the floor of the radio compartment, facing aft in crash-landing positions as required by standard operating procedure. In the rear the scanners reported no obstructions in the way of the huge plane. Barry applied power and the B-36 lurched into motion, rolling into its taxi. Cox called out his checklist of safety and performance indicators as Barry swung Ship

Front view of Convair B-36A. COURTESY USAF

2075 into its takeoff position and applied the brakes. He adjusted the trim and unlocked the flight controls. In all, Ship 2075 had spent only three hours and fifteen minutes on the ground.

Finally, with temperature having risen to the predicted –27°F, Ship 2075 was ready to take to the skies. At 2:27 PM Commander Barry received official clearance and set the brakes before applying thirty seconds of full takeoff power. As the six huge engines accelerated to a deafening throb, he listened for anything out the ordinary. Satisfied that all was as well as could be expected, he released the brakes. The B-36 with its top-secret cargo lumbered down the runway.

The B-36 rumbled down the frozen tarmac, seemingly hesitant to commit itself to the air. Finally, at the end of a long, noisy, heavy-load takeoff, Ship 2075 developed enough lift. Captain Barry later testified

B-36 at takeoff with nose in the air. COURTESY USAF VIA DON PYEATT

that he "had to use full nose-up elevator-trim, plus maximum stick pull-back, to lift the 329,570 pounds of plane and cargo off the runway at 140 miles per hour." Barry had needed almost a mile and a quarter of runway to get airborne. Likely contributing to the long trip down the airstrip was a thin layer of ice that had accumulated on the aircraft caused by ice fog. The running engines had provided some de-icing heat while the plane was on the ground, but Barry later reported that "we took off with a thin skin of ice on the outside panels."

B-36B off the ground. COURTESY USAF

Commander Barry's concerns about the short turnaround were well founded. SAC regulations required all six engines to be running with the propellers turning for takeoff. While technically true for Ship 2075, the hole in the water tank on engine number five meant that the water-injected turbo boost could not be used. Captain Baulch later told investigating officers that "we planned on [using water injection for turbo boost] on takeoff. However, we were getting manifold pressure and torque readings without the water injection system."

As Whitfield operated the controls to retract the landing gear, Cox reported that engine number one, which had not been running at full power, had finally come up to its proper speed. Cox then maintained takeoff power for four minutes. Behind them Ship 2083, one of five training flights scheduled to leave that cold February afternoon, taxied onto the runway.

As Ship 2075 gradually gained altitude, Barry and his crew struggled to complete the repairs left undone by the ground crews at Eielson. The radar and radio operators worked to get their respective sets operating. Darrah squeezed into the wings, trying to set the gas valves in the flight position. Not certain if the B-36 was finally airworthy, Barry swung the plane into a wide circle, buying the crew time to complete the repairs. Ship 2083, in the meantime, left the ground and began its climb. Soon it passed Ship 2075.

Barry later told investigating officers that without the radar and radio working properly, he found it necessary to fly under the cloud cover so he could visually see the ground:

> We were delayed a little bit because I wouldn't go into instrument conditions in the shape the radar set was in and with my radio out. At Anchorage we flew right beneath the base of a cloud. . . . We could see enough to see the ground. We had a little trouble making our position reports on the way down with the stations that didn't have VHF, however [Ship 2083] relayed my reports for me and we worked out OK on that.

The engineers soon discovered other problems. Cox found that he would lose engines number five and six when he attempted to use fuel from the bomb bay tank. The number five cross-feed valve would not operate electronically, and Pooler crawled after Darrah into the wings to manually open it. In the cockpit Barry tried to lose the ice they had picked up. Testifying later, he reported that "we had the anti-icing system on right after takeoff to try to lose some of the ice we had on the airplane when we got it on the ground, and I don't remember whether we had turned that off at any time or not." In fact, they had. In all, at least seven crewmembers spent the first several hours of the flight scrambling to deal with mechanical, electrical and icing problems.

Finally, the crew began reporting to the cockpit that they were solving at least some of the technical troubles. Barry then spent the next six hours coaxing the plane, heavy and traveling at less than 200 knots, to its mission altitude. The crew turned to testing the plane's defensive systems and working the guns as the plane came up to 12,000 feet and went into cruise power.

Almost immediately, new difficulties arose. The engineers were having trouble controlling the engine turbos, and the outside temperature was causing frost to collect on the wings. Cox again turned on the wing anti-icing system to prevent further icing. He then turned the engineer's panel over to Pooler and found room to sit on the steps of the cockpit to write up his log. Within minutes Pooler reported that the plane had lost 10 mph of air speed. Cox had him check with Whitfield, who retrimmed the plane manually in an effort to correct the problem.

Ship 2075 was now fighting a strong headwind, and periodic hail pounded the aircraft. Cox reported that the bomber "had run into a strip of ice. It sounded like sleet, but it was for only a few seconds this continued." Fearing that more ice was forming on the aircraft, Cox ordered the gunners to visually check the outside of the aircraft from their blisters. Normal procedure called for use of the Aldis Lamp, a signaling device that produced a bright, intense burst of light, to check the aircraft surfaces. When asked why the gunners could not see the ice, Cox later testified that the Aldis lamps "were not to be found." The crew pressed themselves against the blister and used flashlights in an attempt to pierce the darkness.

Then the automatic pitch controls for the propellers did not appear to be working, and they began to surge erratically, sending vibrations through the airframe. Pooler believed the problem was caused by icing and increased the engine revolutions to 2,300 to break the ice free. He listened for the sound of ice striking the side of the aircraft as it was dislodged from the propellers. But no ice came off the props.

At the same time, the engineers started "reporting problems with the fuel mixtures in the engines. They were starting to run full-rich. Any attempt to lean them above idle cut-off would fail." Ice was building up in the carburetors. Cox applied carburetor preheat, a system designed to redistribute engine heat to melt the ice. He had not tried to turn on the preheat system earlier because it decreased the power needed to gain altitude. Cox was dismayed to find that the preheat did not work, realizing too late that it had been disconnected on the ground. Later, an unnamed mechanic commenting on the disconnected preheat system, said, "Why not? It didn't work anyway."

Learning that the engine surge was caused by carburetor icing, Barry tried to climb above the icing conditions. He called for an increase in power to 2,650 brake horsepower and 2,550 revolutions, and the climb began. As the bomber rose to about 14,500 feet at the normal climb rate of 155 mph, Cox noted an unusual increase in fuel flow coupled with a decrease in torque. He squeezed his way to the forward blister to get a better idea of what was happening on the outside the B-36.

Finally, just after 11:00 PM, six hours into the flight, Barry finally nursed the aircraft to 15,000 feet. No further climb was possible. The engines continued to run erratically. The operational condition of both the radar and radio remained in doubt. The wings and props were probably coated with ice. The throats of the carburetors were constricting with ice, choking the engines. If Barry had to continue at 15,000 feet to avoid the icing conditions, he risked having to abort his mission because the B-36 was burning too much fuel. For the crew of Ship 2075, it did not seem things could get much worse.

Then all hell broke loose.

CHAPTER FIVE

The Crash of Ship 2075

Hunched in the aft cabin, the left-side rear gunner and scanner, Dick Thrasher, leaned against the observation blister, straining to catch a glimpse of anything in the darkness of the moonless night. Suddenly, at 11:25 PM, a four-foot blue flame erupted from engine number one. An experienced B-36 crewmember, Thrasher was no stranger to engine fires on the big bomber. In an even and controlled voice, he reported the fire to the pilots, who could not see the engines from their seats in the cockpit. Commander Barry ordered the engine shut down and then reduced climb-power to cruise-power to prevent strain on the five remaining engines. Barry was an old hand with B-36 engine failures. Only a few months before in Texas, his number three engine erupted in flames. The blaze was so fierce that the engine fell off the wing, taking the others on that side out. He landed safely under the power of the three engines on the right wing. For Barry and Thrasher, a single engine fire was just another day on a B-36.

Barry contacted Pooler, who, as engineer, controlled the engines during flight. Barry ordered him to feather engine number one. At the official hearing, Engineer Cox testified that "the prop feathered alright. It windmilled backward." The fire went out, but bright red sparks from the engine streaked the night.

Minutes later, Thrasher, still observing the port wing, reported another fire, this time in engine number two. Barry again ordered the engine feathered. Cox had by this time taken over from Pooler at the engineer panel. He feathered number two. The engine fire burned itself out. But like engine number one, sparks traced through the night behind the wing. With two engines out of commission, gravity began to tug,

7th Bomb Wing B-36B, May 1950. Both left-side escape hatches can be seen, one fore and one aft. COURTESY FRANK KLEINWECHTER

and Ship 2075 began losing altitude at a rate of 500 feet per minute (fpm). Unless the crew could slow the rate of descent, Barry knew the B-36 would splash into the water within thirty minutes. Ship 2075 was now in serious jeopardy. With that realization, Barry ordered a broadcast of an emergency distress signal. Because of Ship 2075's radio troubles, sister Ship 2083 relayed the message to Vancouver Air Traffic Control. More messages followed. Each new message became more urgent and added to the details of the airplane's worsening condition. A commercial flight from Langley Airways picked up one of the final messages: "B-36 mayday, water landing between Queen Charlotte Island Sound and Vancouver Island." The bomber was being forced to ditch approximately 200 miles northwest of Vancouver Island.

Then the right-side gunner, Elbert Pollard, reported more bad news to the cockpit. Only seconds after Cox feathered engine number two, number five caught fire. Barry called for Cox to apply emergency power to the remaining three engines. The crew scanned their cockpit and engineering controls, looking for evidence of more power, but even the torque pressure did not increase. The rate of descent had slowed to about 100 fpm, but the airspeed had dropped to a dangerously low 135 mph, only 15 mph above stall speed. Still weighing 135 tons, the crippled B-36

Formation flight of B-36 bombers, showing the view from the left-side rear blister that Gunner Dick Thrasher would have had of the engines on 14 February 1950. Engine number three is shown feathered.
COURTESY FRANK KLEINWECHTER

descended through a gale in darkness, spewing a stream of sparks in its wake. Commander Barry and copilot Whitfield battled against impossibility, trying to keep the giant bomber aloft. The engineers toiled unsuccessfully to get more power from the remaining engines. The radio operator continued to broadcast the Mayday signal, even though the cockpit crew remained uncertain whether the radio was operating.

Whitfield and Thrasher both knew the plane was doomed. Whitfield recalled that they "[s]tarted experiencing multiple failures and none of them could be corrected. Then, when the fires started in the engines, we knew that we had to make plans for leaving the aircraft." Thrasher knew that "[w]hen the three engines caught fire, it was time to leave." The final radio message from Ship 2075 reported that they were 90 miles south of Prince Rupert, British Columbia, and were going to ditch in Queen Charlotte Sound. Ship 2075, with its nuclear payload, was now over Canadian waters.

Weaponeer Ted Schreier had to make the unenviable decision of what to do with the Mark IV atomic bomb nestled in bomb bay number one. Above all he knew he could not allow the American trump card in the Cold War to fall into Soviet hands. Nothing in the standard operating procedures covered such an event, and Schreier had to rely on his training and experience. If he detonated the bomb over land, the bomb's 5,300 pounds of conventional explosives and a hundred pounds of uranium could seriously endanger civilians on the ground. The explosion would not be nuclear, but the conventional explosives and uranium in the bomb would create a dirty bomb and spread radiation in a large radius. To jettison the undetonated bomb over land was unthinkable. The Gouzenko case had proved that Soviet spies were operating in Canada, and Soviet surveillance ships were known to patrol the waters off Canada's coast. Schreier had to make certain the technology packed into the Fat Man's casing remained top secret.

This was not the time to stand on protocol and chain of command. The bomb was Schreier's responsibility, but he polled the busy cockpit crew for their opinions. Each officer, including the observer MacDonald, gave Schreier a reasoned but hurried argument. Whitfield supported dumping the bomb at sea because they were unsure of their position relative to the civilian population on the ground. Barry, MacDonald and Schreier concurred with Whitfield. What other choice did they have? As islands dotting the coast of British Columbia came into radar range as they closed in on the mainland, Barry requested a heading that would take them back out over the open waters of Hecate Strait on the northwest corner of Queen Charlotte Sound. The giant B-36, still pouring sparks into the night air, continued to lose altitude, dropping below 9,000 feet as the waters of the strait appeared below.

Grimly, Schreier headed for bomb bay number one and the Fat Man. He must have known that whatever the outcome, it would not be good for him when—and if—he got back to Carswell AFB. He had signed for the bomb. He was responsible for it, and on the air force's first maximum-effort training mission with the atomic bomb, he was about to dump it over a foreign nation's waters in the dead of night. Whatever action he took, it would be a career-limiting move for a weaponeer serving the intractable General Curtis LeMay.

Inside the falling bomber, Schreier joined Gerhart, already in the bomb bay. Gerhart did not question Schreier's decision. His task was to ensure that the bomb was reduced to fragments at the bottom of the ocean. He moved deeper into the poorly lit bomb bay and grabbed a small aluminum suitcase that held four extra TNT detonators, each the size of a small flashlight. Gerhart checked to ensure that the thirty-two detonators were secure in their predetermined places on the bomb. He verified each in turn, closed the small suitcase on the remaining four spare detonators and slid it back into its assigned place.

Schreier and Gerhart then turned to the next task. The accepted procedure during an accident was to unbolt the birdcage with its plutonium or lead dummy core from the wall of the bomb bay and push it out the bomb bay door. With its parachutes and dinghy, there was a very good chance the core could be recovered before the Soviets found it. If the weaponeer judged that the core could fall into enemy hands, he was to lash the birdcage, with the core safely in its lead-lined container, to the bomb. But with time running short and the ocean rising to meet them, Schreier and Gerhart must have agreed to leave the birdcage bolted to the wall. The last task of the two weapons experts was to set the bomb to explode at an altitude of 3,000 feet. As Gerhart made his way back to his station, he saw Schreier heading back to the cockpit.

Schreier informed Barry and Whitfield that the bomb was ready to jettison. Barry checked their location. They were over Hecate Strait, approximately 140 miles north of Vancouver Island, 50 miles from the nearest land. As the plane descended through 8,000 feet, both Schreier and Barry knew it was now or never. At midnight, 14 February 1950, St. Valentine's Day, Barry ordered the weapon jettisoned.

Whitfield hit the salvo switch to open the bomb bay door and drop the bomb. Nothing happened. He hit the switch again. The door under bomb bay number one finally slid up the left side the bomber. The catches snapped open and the huge 10,000-pound Mark IV slipped into the darkness. Around 3,000 feet above the water, the thirty-two detonators exploded, igniting the 5,300 pounds of conventional explosives in the bomb's shell. Shrouded in fog and low clouds, the bomb lit the night sky like a bulb inside a shade. Radioactive fragments showered down into Hecate Strait and sank to the ocean floor.

B-36 with all four bomb bay doors partially open. COURTESY USAF

Several crew members both saw and felt the explosion. Whitfield recalled seeing the flash as it exploded, and Dick Thrasher remembered seeing the clouds light up. While Gerhart rigged his parachute, shock waves from the blast rocked the B-36 and knocked him off balance.

Commander Barry ordered the crew to bail out. Whitfield gave the emergency signal to the crew—three short rings on the alarm bells—and the crew now turned to saving themselves.

Barry knew he had to pilot the crippled bomber back over land if the crew were to have any hope of survival. Parachuting into the frigid winter waters of the Pacific Ocean would result in hypothermia within a matter of minutes. A controlled landing in the water was not a choice because air force brass had decided "it would be better to bail out over water than try to ditch the aircraft." To back it up, they had ordered the removal of all six-person life rafts from the B-36 fleet. Even if standard procedure had allowed for the attempt, gale-force conditions and high seas made such a maneuver unlikely to succeed. "The radar operator gave me a heading to take me back over land (northeast on a bearing perpendicular to the coast)," Barry testified later. "The engineer gave me emergency power to try to hold our altitude. We still descended quite rapidly and by the time we got over land we were at 5,000 feet."

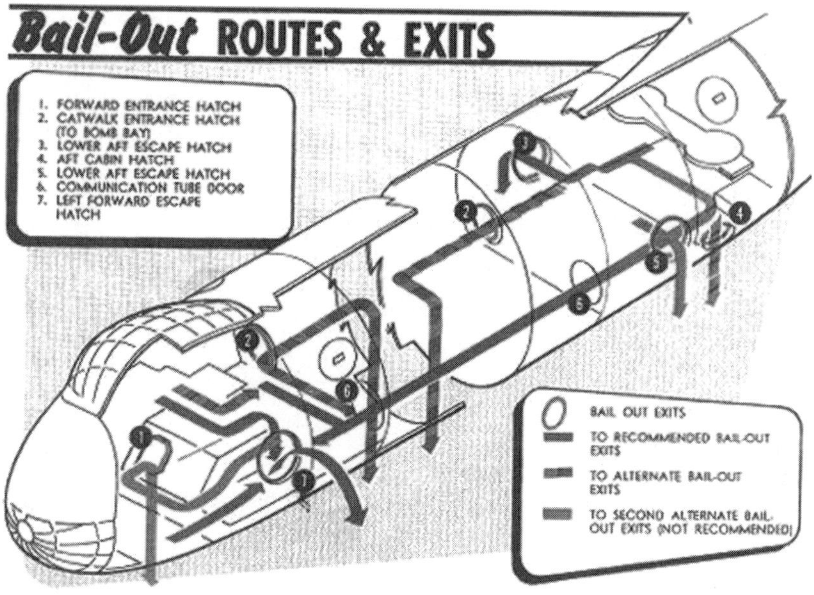

Bailout routes and exits on the B-36. COURTESY USAF

The B-36 sputtered toward the coast of central British Columbia. Islands dappled the Pacific Ocean off the coast like pieces of a jigsaw puzzle. They were all sizes, ranging from minuscule rocky outcrops to large landmasses with deep rain forest and towering mountains. As the stricken bomber continued northeast, Gerhart reported that "they were over land, then over water, then land again, more water, and more land." As the much larger Princess Royal Island hove into view on the radar, Barry nudged the aircraft to a heading slightly east of south and into the strong 55-knot headwind.

Separated from the mainland by the narrow Princess Royal Channel and occupying 876 square miles, Princess Royal Island is 325 miles north of Vancouver. Fiords carve deeply into the west coast of the island, estuaries serrate the coastline and lakes dot the interior. Flying at 5,000 feet and losing altitude quickly, Barry was most concerned about the possibility of crashing into the island's mountains.

As Barry nursed the doomed bomber, Whitfield prepared the crew for bail out. "From my position in the cockpit," he recounted, "it appeared that the crew was functioning normally while making preparations to leave the aircraft. They had been trained to follow procedures for this and they were doing their jobs. They put on their parachutes and removed the observation blisters from the sides of the plane to provide openings from which to exit." Whitfield checked each man in the front compartment to ensure he had rigged his Mae West life preserver and parachute straps correctly.

Back in the rear compartment, Stephens was rushing the crew through the same bailout procedure. Thrasher found it "too difficult to get the damned Mae West straps under so I unfastened my chute in front, threw it back, got a Mae West and put it on, but my own chute was so tight in front that I fastened it under the Mae West." The crew had no time to don exposure suits, but Thrasher pulled his parka from his bunk and pushed it through a loose leg strap. The gunners in the back fastened dinghies to one another. Thrasher recalled that "[t]here was some doubt as to whether we would be able to make it to the island or not, so we fastened these on to one another quick. It is rather difficult to sit in a blister with a parachute and dinghy on. It put you up so high you break your back leaning over." Back in the forward compartment, Ford screwed down the transmitter key on his radio in an effort to give rescuers a steady signal to locate the downed bomber. In the meantime Barry hurried the crew. Outside the three-foot diameter escape hatches waited fog, a driving rain, a 55-knot wind, and—somewhere, they hoped—land and safety.

The end had come. Barry knew the parachutes needed a thousand feet of altitude to slow the men's descents. Even now, closing in on the mountains, it was hard to guarantee that they would have that minimum. "The radar operator told me that there was terrain which in a few places ran up to 3,500 feet and that is one reason I wanted [the crew] out. I rang the alarm bell and told them to leave—I ordered the crew to bail out, and away they went." Barry did not mention whether he shut down engine number three on the same side of the aircraft as the escape hatches as called for by standard operating procedure. However, it is probable he did to avoid the risk of the crew leaping into the 19-foot propeller.

The first to jump from the front compartment were Phillips and Ascol, followed by Cox, Ford, Schuler, Trippodi, Pooler, MacDonald and Gerhart. Gerhart shot under engine number two. Sparks from the burning engine pelted his face. When he pulled the ripcord, nothing happened. He frantically pulled the parachute out of its pack by hand. The rain soaked his face as the high winds swung him like a pendulum beneath his canopy. Princess Royal Island rushed up to meet him.

In the rear compartment, Thrasher received the order to abandon ship. "[Barry] said we were over Princess Royal Island, and to go ahead and bail out." Thrasher and the others "went out the rear entrance hatch . . . on the bottom of the left side." Gunners Straley and Pollard exited first. Thrasher was next. "Stephens told us that in exiting the plane, jumping technique was important," recalled Thrasher. "Straley, the first to jump, followed official procedures and rolled out in a tight crouch. His pack (which included the parachute and one-man life raft) got hooked on the rim of the small hatch. Stephens kicked him loose. Pollard, who went next, had previously bailed out of a disabled aircraft. . . . He knew what he was doing and ignored the rules; he simply dove out head first."

"This was my first time to bail out," Thrasher said in his later testimony to the official inquiry. "I have always been told that you are to get your feet at the near edge of the opening and try to roll out in a ball, so as not to bang your head against the plane or injure yourself." Having watched Pollard successfully exit the plane, Thrasher still followed procedure and tried to roll out in a crouch. He too got wedged in the small opening. Thrasher would owe a debt of gratitude to Stephens. "Stephens kicked me free. He saved my life." Thrasher struggled to get his parachute opened, his ripcord pinned under his Mae West. Hurtling toward the ground, he tore off a glove and worked his fingers into the metal handle. Finally, after what felt like an eternity, the chute billowed open above his head. Thrasher remembered that he "was well down by this time, but [he] still had a few minutes to think things over before [he] hit." The last to exit the rear of the plane were Darrah and Stephens.

Ship 2075 lurched through the winter night toward the mountain peaks at the center of Princess Royal Island. The ocean was receding behind them, and the three remaining officers—Barry, Whitfield and Schreier—had to bail out quickly or risk landing far inland in the rugged, mountainous terrain. Parachuting near the coast represented their best hope for survival and rescue. They fumbled with their parachutes and emergency equipment in the shadows of the cramped forward cabin. Whitfield checked the rigging of his fellow officers as they checked his. Whitfield recalled that he "pointed out to the other copilot, Captain Schreier, that he had his floatation vest on over his parachute." Whitfield then saw Schreier "hurriedly removing his vest." Schreier had just seen his career fall from the airplane and explode spectacularly above the Pacific. Now he had to re-rig his parachute in near darkness on the world's largest bomber as it fell from the sky.

Barry ordered Schreier and Whitfield to bail out, then rushed up the short flight of steps that connected the upper and lower decks of the forward compartment. As a pilot, Schreier knew the drill. Barry was setting the autopilot on a heading to take the bomber back out over the sea, where it would crash beyond the hands of the prying Soviets. Barry set the automatic pilot for "a gentle clockwise curve which he estimated would ditch the plane somewhere in Queen Charlotte Sound. The time was five minutes past midnight."

Schreier edged away from the open escape hatch, wrestling with his parachute and Mae West rigging. Perhaps his motive was to keep the escape route clear for Barry and Whitfield in case their situation worsened quickly. Perhaps the low ceiling and crowded forward compartment near the escape hatch made it too difficult to re-rig his parachute and Mae West. Whatever his motive, he likely headed for the elbow room and the higher ceiling near the radio compartment just a few feet away. The clock ticked, each second marking the passage of a few more feet closer to the ground. Schreier would have felt the giant B-36 list as it began its gentle clockwise turn. He would have known he had only a few minutes at best to readjust his gear before the bomber's new course took it back out over the icy waters of Queen Charlotte Sound. Sometime before Barry's return from the cockpit, Whitfield bailed out. Whitfield recalled, "As I jumped I rolled over so that I could see the plane pass over me before my chute opened. I saw a brilliant blue/white streamer of fire trailing one engine for as far back as the tail of the plane." As he drifted down, Whitfield realized that he had not seen Schreier jump. "No one knows if he did or did not jump," he would later remark.

Lower nose compartment of the B-36. In the left foreground is the navigator and to his left, the photo navigator. In the nose is the gunner and weather observer, and to his right is the radar observer. COURTESY USAF

As Commander Barry made his way down from the flight deck after setting the autopilot, the top-heavy bulkiness of his parachute and Mae West would likely have forced him to back down the steps to the lower deck. He would have had his back to the radio compartment and would not have seen Schreier if he was indeed there. As Barry reached the escape hatch, he scanned what he could see of the forward compartment. It was empty. As commander of the aircraft, he had a duty to be the last to leave. Relieved that all the crew had bailed out, Barry rolled out of the hatch. "I didn't jump hard enough," he remembered. "I just kind of stuck my head out and expected to fall out, and the wind pressure held me to the escape hatch, but I cleared the propeller by a good many feet." As Barry's parachute opened, he was jerked upward in the strong wind.

Unknown to Barry, Schreier still struggled with the straps and buckles on his Mae West and parachute in the near darkness of the radio compartment. As he fought his way back to the escape hatch, he

The radio observer's position on the RB-36. COURTESY USAF

must have wondered where the veering plane had taken him. The wind howled through the narrow hatch, and rain lashed against the fuselage. In the overcast, moonless night, he stared into the darkness. What waited below? The rugged mass of Princess Royal Island? Or the gale-whipped whitecaps of the sea? His heart must have sunk as he calculated that the B-36 was well into its gentle turn over Whale Channel, off the west coast of the island. In his mind's eye, mountains must have receded in the distance as the ocean opened below. He must known he had missed his chance. If he jumped now, he would land in the Pacific with virtually no chance of survival.

With jumping no longer an option, Schreier would have turned his thoughts to other alternatives for survival. He had flown bombers throughout World War II. He had often been at the controls of the B-36. He was a skilled navigator. Schreier had attended the B-36 training sessions presented by Beryl Erickson, the test pilot for the B-36, who had told the class that despite its great size and mechanical complexity, the B-36 was as easy to handle as any World War II bomber. His instincts as a pilot would have kicked in. Schreier headed up the steps to the cockpit and dropped into the pilot's seat. He was about to find out if Erickson was right.

Schreier had two problems to deal with immediately: he had to get back over Princess Royal Island, where he could to jump to safety, and he had to stop losing altitude. Schreier knew that without the application of additional power, the turn set on the autopilot would cause the bomber to approximately double its 100-fpm rate of descent, but he could not control engine power or have access to radar readings from the pilot's seat. Schreier must have run the numbers in his head: he had little more than twenty minutes before the plane's long arc plunged it into Queen Charlotte Sound.

Schreier would also have known that the best way to increase lift and gain altitude was to turn the bomber into the 55-knot wind. He needed to reverse the autopilot's clockwise turn to take the giant bomber back over Princess Royal Island, but he must have wondered if the route would take him dangerously close to the mountains before he could gain altitude. Schreier made his decision. He switched off the autopilot and reversed the clockwise turn. Barry later testified that he instinctively looked up to follow the course of the B-36 as he parachuted toward the island. "The ship was on automatic pilot and somehow it turned in the air and came back over us. There were three engines burning and I could follow the ship's progress as I went down in my chute. But I don't know where she crashed." Whitfield also testified that he observed the aircraft change course to a counterclockwise direction while under the canopy of his parachute. Whitfield, too, recalled seeing the engines still trailing sparks in the dark night sky.

Whitfield stated in a letter interview that he saw only one man jump from the plane after him. Later, on the ground, he would conclude that Schreier had not jumped. Thrasher, already on the ground, confirmed their testimony.

Perhaps Schreier reasoned he could pilot the bomber back over the island to allow him to jump in the same area as the rest of the crew. But without a radar operator to confirm the plane's position, he could not have known his exact location in relation to the crew members already on the ground. At best he could have roughly estimated his position. Further, as a thorough professional and patriot, Schreier knew his duty was to reset the autopilot on a course that would cause the bomber to crash out at sea. The autopilot took several minutes to engage after a course had been set. Even if he found the island, he would have to engage the autopilot, wait for it to lock in, make it to the escape hatch and jump—all within the few minutes the plane would be over what he hoped was the island's coast near the other crewmembers.

As the plane turned into the wind, Schreier must have realized that Erickson had been right: the B-36 was a handful to fly solo but no more than World War II bombers. Even with a lone pilot at the controls, the spring tabs mounted on the trailing edges of the control surfaces allowed them to move with ease.

For whatever reason Schreier missed his second chance to jump. The B-36 continued out to sea. If he circled yet again, the aircraft would lose even more altitude, and he would be too low to parachute. The best place to be was over the Pacific, where he would have time to consider his other options. Whatever Schreier's thoughts and motives at the moment, he did not reengage the autopilot. He straightened out the B-36 on a northwest heading out over Queen Charlotte Sound.

Schreier must have considered the odds of the dwindling number of survival options remaining. He no doubt knew he would not need to worry about burning too much fuel because the bomber carried enough for a twenty-hour flight plus a reserve. When Barry had ordered the crew to bail out, they had been in the air just over six hours. Schreier would have fourteen hours of fuel to reach safety if he could keep the B-36 aloft. Schreier may have wondered if the carburetor icing problem

B-36 flying low over the water. COURTESY USAF

of the bomber's three remaining engines had abated in the warmer and drier air over the island. He may have considered reengaging the autopilot to allow him to check both the engine controls and the radio, neither of which he could see or operate from the pilot's seat. He may have weighed the possibility of sending out a voice transmission, but he had no idea if the radio was functioning.

Schreier must have recognized that his only option for survival was to put the bomber back on the ground. He might have asked, "What would General LeMay do?" The answer: "Bring it on home." He could head south on their mission coordinates, but the runways of the nearest airport, Vancouver International, over 300 miles to the south, could not accommodate the B-36. The next nearest SAC base with a suitable runway was Fairchild AFB at Spokane, Washington, 393 miles beyond Vancouver. Charting a course to Spokane would give Schreier a chance to gain altitude flying into the wind, but if the ailing bomber lost more power, he might crash into a populated area. Worse, traveling along the coast where the worst fogs formed would risk further icing of the carburetors. Eielson AFB was much farther to the north. However, the northern flight path would take him over the drier and warmer air of the interior of northern British Columbia—and, most importantly, it would take the B-36 away from Soviet spy boats suspected to be patrolling the coastal waters off Canada.

Schreier eased the B-36 into a gentle right-hand turn, guiding it to a northeast bearing. Setting the course would be easy enough. It wasn't the first time Schreier had flown a plane using a compass and dead reckoning. Without radar he would have to stay below the clouds. Schreier may have gained confidence, but he knew he had to gain altitude, too. Mountain ridges over 6,000 feet high lay between him and Eielson. Peering into the darkness as he winged over Queen Charlotte Sound, Schreier would have seen only the faint fluorescence of cresting waves beneath him, then the dark outlines of the small islands that dotted the British Columbia coast. For approximately the next two hours, Schreier continued his course toward the northeast. Back over land, the relative humidity and the temperature dropped, reducing the amount of moisture in the air. The skies cleared and he flew by starlight. The carburetor icing abated, and he gained power. The burning of fuel lightened the load and helped him gain altitude. He managed to climb over the first mountain ridges between him and Eielson. Before him was a patchwork of various shades of black and gray. Complete blackness meant mountains; lighter patches meant safe passage through the peaks.

Just before 3:00 AM, only 300 miles from the Alaska border, Schreier encountered his last obstacle. If he could get over this hurdle, a broad valley opened up to lead him to safety. But the bomber, for whatever reasons, had lost approximately 500 feet of altitude since cresting the previous range. Above the Pacific, 500 feet would be of little consequence. Here it could prove fatal, and Schreier knew it. He pulled back on the yoke, trying to coax more altitude from the plane. The three remaining engines had nothing left to give. Ship 2075 refused to respond. As the saddle of Mount Kologet loomed before him, Schreier's field of vision shrunk to blackness. As he struggled at the controls, darkness completely filled the windscreen of Ship 2075 as the plane met the mountain. The aircraft struck the glacier on an angle and skidded up the mountain. The tail slammed into the snow and rock-hard ice. The impact tore the airframe apart. The nose buried into the glacier 75 feet below the crest of the saddle. At 3:05 AM on Valentine's Day 1950, the distress signal on Ship 2075 went dead.

Schreier came within a few feet, a few minutes and a few miles of home and safety. U.S. ground stations monitoring the plane's signal breathed a sigh of relief, believing their most closely guarded military secret was now sinking beneath the waters of the Pacific. In fact, it was buried in the ice and snow of a remote glacier high in the Canadian wilderness.

CHAPTER SIX

The Search for Ship 2075

When the radio operator screwed down the transmitter key on his radio before he bailed out, he hoped his radio was working and rescue crews would track the universal distress signal and search for the aircrew. It worked. The Royal Canadian Air Force (RCAF) station at Sea Island, near Vancouver International Airport, picked up the bomber's distress call. Within minutes they launched a rescue mission code-named Operation Brix. Aircraft from the 123rd Search and Rescue Squadron, along with two U.S. helicopters, were quickly scouring the area for the giant bomber and its crew, with other aircraft joining the search within hours.

The evening edition of the *Vancouver Daily Province* broke the news on the same day the B-36 went missing. Under a banner headline STORM HIDES FATE OF B-36, 17 MEN. FLAMING BOMBER DOWN OFF B.C. COAST, the paper ran a photo of a B-36. A highly placed source must have advised the newspapers that Ship 2075 was carrying two extra crew members. The *Vancouver Sun* also carried a detailed account of the efforts to find the survivors, who were believed to be in the ocean because the plane had been sent on a course out to sea:

> Forty Canadian and U.S. air-sea rescue craft fought today through gale winds and rain off the north tip of Vancouver Island in a massive search for a lost B-36 bomber and its crew of 17. The giant plane, with one engine ablaze and another acting badly, splashed into the sea at about 3:30 AM today while winging southward along the B.C. coast from Alaska bound for Texas. Gales up to 40 miles an hour envelope the search scene in Queen

> Charlotte Sound. Survivors, if any, would be clinging to life rafts, drenched by charging seas, and their chances for survival are uncertain. But a huge two-nation search force was speeding to the scene. Thirty-four planes, including seven Vancouver-based RCAF craft and 10 B-29 Superfortresses are covering the area from the air.

The story was out. Now the U.S. Air Force (USAF) tried to control the spin. Major General Roger Ramey explained to journalists that "the plane had been on a routine training flight." He never mentioned, of course, the existence of the Mark IV nuclear weapon or its core, plutonium or otherwise.

Miles to the southeast of the area where Operation Brix searched for the lost B-36, the survivors organized themselves on Princess Royal Island as best they could. Bounded by narrow beaches that led to lowland rain forests and alpine tundra on the high mountains, the remote island could not have been more inhospitable. Estuaries, lakes and salt marshes punctuated the terrain. The survivors had landed in a line that ran from the shore to almost 3 miles inland. Pooler, first of the survivors to jump, landed approximately a mile from the coast. Barry, the last to jump, landed the farthest inland.

Dick Thrasher had tried to avoid the trees that dotted his landing area. It didn't work. "I landed in a tree and hung up," he reported. "It was dark, and I could feel a big branch with my foot. Not knowing how far above the ground I was, I thought I better stay put. As my eyes got used to the dark, I could see the branch. It was a big tree root. I was on the ground. I cut myself free with a knife." As he tumbled into the hip-deep snow, he witnessed the bomber circle back over him.

Gerhart, too, landed in a tree, his feet just touching the ground. He opened one parachute strap, but had to use his knife to cut away the other when it jammed. He fell forward, landing in 3 feet of soft snow. Reaching over his head, he pulled his parachute from the tree. Gerhart did a quick inventory of his survival gear: a cigarette lighter, some matches, four candles, a can of lighter fluid, a knife, forty rounds of ammunition, a .45 Savage automatic, an extra pair of gloves, a compass, all of his heavy arctic clothing and a pair of Eskimo mukluks.

Gerhart lit a candle. He called out and was surprised to receive an answer from nearby. It was good to know he was not alone. He shouted for the other man to stay where he was while he found him. Gathering up his parachute, Gerhart stumbled his way downhill in the darkness, fighting through the deep snow. Suddenly, he felt himself falling before landing heavily about 10 feet below. Stunned, he rolled slowly onto his back. Cold rain pelted his face. He cleared his head and relit his candle. He had fallen into a ravine. He called out to the other man that they should both stay put and wait for morning. It would be safer for both of them. Gerhart wrapped himself in his parachute and tried to sleep.

Commander Barry landed in the water but thankfully not the ocean. "I landed in a little pond with a thin ice crust on it," he reported. He was possibly 2 miles or better inland. He testified, "Colonel MacDonald landed nearby and we walked off of it. Along the shoreline about 3 feet had melted through. Lt [Darrah], who was the last man out of the rear, landed within shouting distance of me."

Whitfield landed in the trees like Thrasher. "My chute snagged in a tree and I hung there for several minutes," he recalled. "It was dark and foggy and I couldn't see the ground. I hung there for a while until my chute ripped and dropped me and snagged a lower branch. I could still not see the ground. As my eyes adjusted I could see the snow beneath me so I released the chute first from the lower part of the harness and then from the top. I fell onto a steep slope and started rolling downhill." Compared to some of the others, he recounted, "I had it easy. I never thought it could be so simple. I didn't even get scratched. In the morning I saw there were sharp stumps and trees all around me, but I had missed them all." Nevertheless, Whitfield, like the others, suffered from the cold, wet conditions. Whitfield later recalled the crew:

> had the typical survival kits of that time. This included chocolate bars, a first-aid kit, a knife, some water and other items. We were still wearing our "dry" suits. The plan called for us to change into "wet" suits during the flight, but we had not done so. The dry suits were made of a porous material that would "breathe" to allow for

air circulation and drying of perspiration. This proved to be a major problem for all of us because our clothes soon filled with water, and we remained cold and wet until we were rescued.

Whitfield climbed uphill to an overhang that gave him shelter from the alternating snow and rain. To conserve his matches, he decided not to start a fire, opting instead to wrap himself in his parachute. For Whitfield things didn't seem so bad: "We were all as lucky as the day is long. It was nothing short of a miracle."

Thrasher fared even better. He inflated his one-man rubber dinghy, crawled under it and went to sleep. The raft kept him dry through the night. Barry saw things very differently. "I got pretty wet and so did my chute. It didn't do me much good for warmth during the rest of the night. I tried to build a fire but couldn't."

Pooler also ended up in the trees. Releasing the straps on his parachute, he fell over 40 feet, breaking his right ankle. In excruciating pain he limped over a mile down the mountainside to a frozen lake, where he settled in to wait for rescue.

The survivor in the greatest difficulty was radioman Trippodi, who came down in a treetop near the peak of a steep incline. "I was hanging there in that tree," he remembered, "head down with a foot caught in a chute strap. I had lost my right strap on the jump. When I first landed in the tree, I tried to shake myself loose. I then fell headfirst. That's when my foot caught. If I hadn't lost that right strap, I would have had something to grab, and never would have got hung up." Trippodi, suffering from numerous injuries, including a broken ankle, would hang upside down, exposed to the elements, for twelve hours.

The morning of Valentine's Day 1950 dawned cold, gray and wet. Barry's first order of the day was to satisfy his gnawing hunger. Spotting a ground squirrel standing on a fallen tree a few yards away, he drew his .45-caliber pistol and fired twice, missing both times. As the squirrel raced away to safety, Barry was surprised to hear a survival whistle being blown repeatedly. It was Whitfield, who was up early and searching for a route to the coast. Whitfield's survival training dictated that he find a stream and follow it downhill to the coast, where it would be much easier for rescue planes and ships to spot him. Soon he saw Barry walking toward him. The two men had a brief reunion and then moved downhill.

Pooler, well below Barry and Whitfield, stayed put on the shore. Using a search and rescue signaling mirror, he tried to catch the attention of a rescue aircraft circling overhead. Twice the plane passed over him and twice he saw the light from the mirror dancing on the fuselage. But the rescue crew never saw his signal and flew away.

Gerhart awoke to the shouts of the man he had tried to find the night before. The voice was coming from somewhere below him. Gerhart picked up his parachute and in the cold dawn worked his way toward the sound. He found Ford, who, like Gerhart, was cold and tired, but otherwise fine. Ford had even less survival gear than Gerhart: a magazine, some matches, a pack of cigarettes, a lighter and four signal flares. The men knew they had to find the coast. They packed up their parachutes, fastened Ford's one-man raft onto his back and picked their way down the mountain, following a stream they hoped would lead them to the water's edge. Soon tired from their exertions, they gathered some dead wood and started a fire. The fire kept dying out, and Ford poured more and more lighter fluid on it to keep it going. Not long after, they heard gunshots followed by shouts coming from all around them. Gerhart fired two answering shots. Then he and Ford called out for the next two hours, hoping other survivors would find them. When no one arrived and the weather closed in, they once again started for the coast.

Dick Thrasher woke up cold and stiff. "I climbed the tree to try to get my chute. I wanted to wrap myself in it." While in the tree, he called out and recognized the voice of Ford. Making his way toward the sound of Ford's voice, Thrasher picked his way through the rocks and deadfall, aiming at what appeared to be small clearings. The clearings turned out to be ponds covered in slush. Thinking that it would be easier to row across the ponds than walk, he inflated his life raft. But he had to abandon it when he realized it was impossible to row through the slush. Climbing over a large deadfall, he finally found Ford and was happy to find Gerhart there as well.

The three men decided scout the immediate area for other survivors. Soon they found Stephens and MacDonald. Their group had grown to five. Weak from their ordeal, the men abandoned their efforts to reach the coast and used the raft and parachutes to build a makeshift shelter. They tried to start a fire but could not find any dry wood because of the incessant rain. They emptied their pockets of any dry paper, including Ford's magazine, and finally, using their lighters and some lighter fluid, they got the fire going. Soon the men heard a plane flying high overhead. They piled green boughs on the fire, hoping to create enough smoke to alert the observers searching for them. It was not enough. The plane turned and disappeared. As night fell, the men tried to bolster their morale by predicting that the searchers would be back soon. Their second night was just as cold and wet as the first.

As Barry and Whitfield crashed through the dense undergrowth toward the coast, they discovered Trippodi hanging from a tree. "After perhaps an hour of stepping through crusty snow and ice into the water underneath we heard a shout. After a lengthy search we spotted Trippodi hanging upside down." The two officers spent over two hours extricating the radioman from the tree. Trippodi's broken ankle and frostbitten feet meant he would not be able to walk to the coast. Whitfield and Barry found a dry recess in the rocks and made a bed of tree branches. Though exhausted, they dragged Trippodi to the makeshift shelter. While Whitfield built a fire, Barry put Trippodi's feet under his own jacket to warm them and restart the circulation. By 9:00 PM the driving rain put their fire out. The three men huddled under their parachutes, trying to keep one another warm. Barry grew more and more worried because Trippodi was running a fever and was almost delirious from shock.

As dawn broke on the morning of 15 February, Barry and Whitfield moved out of Trippodi's earshot to discuss their situation. If the three men were to survive, Barry and Whitfield would have to find the coast, where the chance of being spotted was better. Then they could then send help for Trippodi. The thought of leaving Trippodi weighed heavily on both officers. "The decision for both of us going was based on our survival training that taught us to never strike out alone to find help," recalled Whitfield. "A single person will often not survive the journey." Barry and Whitfield gave Trippodi the bad news. "[They] told me that they couldn't stay with me," Trippodi recollected. "They had to go find help for the others, but they would come back for me." Trippodi felt very, very alone as he watched Barry and Whitfield disappear through the trees.

Gerhart and his group decided that they, too, had to continue toward the coast to improve their chance of rescue. "We were a couple of miles from the shore," Thrasher recalled. "When morning came, we decided to try to walk." For the benefit of the rescuers who would be looking for them, Gerhart marked a large X in the snow with dye from his survival kit and drew an arrow pointed at the coast. The going was tough. Every thirty minutes, a new man took the lead to break trail through the snow. Fearing exhaustion, the group stopped every 200 yards to rest before pushing on. Heading slowly westward the men finally crested a hill and saw the Pacific Ocean below them. They pushed on, their morale boosted. The group discovered two sets of human tracks leading to a fast-moving stream bridged by a fallen log. Knowing that only fellow crew members could have made the tracks, they crawled across the log and picked up the trail again on the other side. The tracks led them closer and closer to the coast. Near the water's edge, the group found Barry and Whitfield. The two officers had already stamped out an SOS in the snow and filled the impressions with green boughs to make the message more visible from the air. All seven were soaked to the skin and suffering from the early stages of hypothermia, so Whitfield started a fire. Soon everyone was gathering wood to build the fire higher. They were playing it by the book: they had found an open spot, stamped out a signal, stayed together and built a fire.

Thrasher recounts that several hours later they "heard a motor. At first it sounded like a plane, then we decided it was a boat." Silence fell as they waited to see if their ears were playing tricks. Then everyone reacted at the same moment. They fired flares, jumped up and down and shouted—anything to get the boat crew's attention. The boat sailed on, disappearing behind a point of land.

Fifteen minutes later another boat appeared and just as quickly disappeared behind a small island. The men became despondent and began to entertain the prospect of dying on this remote island in central British Columbia.

The HMCS Cayuga, *which assisted in the search for the downed aircrew of Ship 2075.* COURTESY CANADIAN DEPARTMENT OF NATIONAL DEFENCE

On the afternoon of 15 February, the 72-foot Canadian fish packer *Cape Perry* made its way through the coastal waters en route to the herring grounds in Queen Charlotte Sound. Like the skipper of every other boat and aircraft in the area, the *Cape Perry*'s captain, Vance King, was following the news of the search for Ship 2075 when he heard reports that the search was now centering on Princess Royal Island. King altered course to run closer to the shore. At noon the spotters on the *Cape Perry* reported seeing smoke rising. King ordered a small rowboat ashore to investigate. The rescuers found Cox, Darrah and Schuler. The rowboat returned to the *Cape Perry* with three very happy B-36 crew members. King helped the Americans settle in and returned to the helm. As he revved the engine and swung the boat away from shore, someone spotted another wisp of smoke. Once again he dispatched the rowboat to investigate. King's crew found Barry and his group huddled around their fire. The rowboat ferried the men to the *Cape Perry*. King was proud of his crew. "I felt pretty good about getting those guys out," he recalled. "We had a bottle of rum and a bottle of Scotch aboard and gave them some drinks. Then we gave them some ham and eggs and put them to bed aboard our boat. I never saw a braver bunch of men. I know I wouldn't bail out of any

Canso like the one that took the crew back to the U.S. from Vancouver Island (this one painted in the USAF colors). COURTESY DAVID LEGGE

ship, let alone in a gale, at midnight." Thrasher summed up the thoughts of the crew of the B-36: "The Canadians really treated us fine. . . . I was really happy to see that boat, for I fully expected to spend another night in the snow."

Barry informed King of the location and condition of Trippodi and asked King to alert the search parties. The Canadian destroyer *Cayuga* responded to King's call for help. As the ship waited offshore, a mountain-rescue team searched inland. The Canadians quickly located the radio operator high on the mountain, nearly dead from exposure. They began the difficult job of carrying him back to the *Cayuga*.

Trippodi felt he was living a miracle:

> When my pilot and my co-pilot pulled me down Tuesday, and left me lying there, I felt like I was dead. When they left me, I wanted to go too. I was afraid they would get lost and nobody ever would find me. I laid there I don't know how long. Those Canadians who picked me up were the swellest people I ever met. The first thing they did was to give me morphine to kill the pain in my foot. Then I drank all their cocoa.

Trippodi would recover from all of his injuries.

Finally, on the morning of Thursday, 16 February, the crew of the *Cayuga* found Pooler. The search party called out his name again and again, and finally heard him calling back. His fifty-four-hour ordeal was over. He had survived on a single candy bar he had purchased before climbing aboard the C-54 at Carswell on 2 February. "I remember digging out that candy bar and counting the squares and figuring out that if I ate one square of chocolate a day, I could eat for nine days."

Five men remained missing: Straley and Pollard, who had bailed out first from the rear of the B-36, Phillips and Ascol, who had jumped first from the front compartment, and Schreier, who, based on the landing pattern of the others should have set down between Whitfield and Barry. The search team from the *Cayuga* found two parachutes in the trees and footprints in the snow. It is believed these belonged to the already rescued men. Four days later the search crews found another parachute, a Mae West and a radar reflector. Near the reflector an SOS had been stamped in the snow. It is believed this was the location of Pooler's rescue. The next day small personal items were found, but then Princess Royal Island went silent. None of the missing was ever found.

Stephens was haunted by the deaths of Straley and Pollard. Thrasher confided that "Stephens blamed himself for [their] deaths . . . but it wasn't his fault. It really bothered him—if he hadn't been in such a hurry to get them out, they might have survived. After a while, he wouldn't talk about it anymore."

The ten men rescued by the *Cape Perry* were flown to Port Hardy at the extreme northern end of Vancouver Island. There the media was waiting, and soon photos of the rescued crew were in newspapers around the world. Trippodi and Pooler were flown directly to a USAF hospital at McChord AFB near Tacoma, Washington. As the Canso landed, Strategic Air Command, obsessed with security, ordered the U.S. Coast Guard to inform all involved with the rescue to "Handle this with care. Pass [the survivors] on without interrogation. Again, handle this with care. No leaks." When the transport plane carrying them back to Carswell AFB lost an engine on landing, the survivors received one more vivid reminder why flying in the 1950s was still a very hazardous occupation. Despite arriving safely, Gerhart would claim, "That's when some of us seriously thought, 'To hell with it.'"

Twelve crewmembers survived the ordeal on Valentine's Day 1950. Four crewmembers were missing and presumed dead in the Pacific. The fate of Schreier remained a mystery.

CHAPTER SEVEN

Ship 2075 Rediscovered

THE LOSS OF THE WORLD'S LARGEST AND MOST SOPHISTICATED BOMBER was big news. That it was carrying a nuclear bomb was potentially devastating news, and the U.S. Air Force (USAF) began its first-ever effort to hide the trail to the truth of the fate of a lost nuclear bomb. The weapon, the aircraft and the mission were top secret. As newspapers reported the sighting of an oil slick off Princess Royal Island, USAF Major General Roger Ramey informed journalists that a bomber had crashed on a routine training flight, making no mention of a nuclear bomb aboard. His statement would become the standard U.S. response to media questions about the loss of nuclear weapons in the future. Henceforth, when asked about the presence of nuclear weapons, military spokespersons would answer, "It is U.S. policy neither to confirm nor deny the presence or absence of nuclear weapons at any specific location." If questioned about nuclear weapons aboard a specific vessel or aircraft, the answer to this day is: "It is general U.S. policy not to deploy nuclear weapons aboard surface ships, attack submarines and naval aircraft. However, we do not discuss the presence or absence of nuclear weapons aboard specific ships, submarines or aircraft."

Ramey's statement held the press and public at bay for a while, and his silence about the bomb gave nothing away to potential Soviet snoopers. But the Atomic Energy Commission (AEC) wanted answers. After all, it was their nuclear bomb that was missing. Bill Sheehy, an AEC official, wrote a memo to his boss, William Borden, Executive Director of the Joint Committee on Atomic Energy. "I am not willing to sit back and wait until the air force gets damn good and ready to tell us what the hell they did with one of our atomic weapons," he stated bluntly. In response to the pressure from Sheehy, Borden demanded information from the air force on 9 March 1950. Major General Thomas White responded that "the bomb was jettisoned, presumably over the sea, and it exploded while in the air. Its mechanism was set to

The British Columbia wilderness as seen from Mount Kologet, where Ship 2075 was eventually discovered. COURTESY DOUG DAVIDGE

detonate the charge at approximately 3,800 feet." The lack of absolute certainty was hardly comforting. White confirmed the bomb did not contain the plutonium core when it was destroyed.

The air force immediately convened a top-secret board of inquiry to investigate the crash of Ship 2075. Three members of the crew—Commander Barry, Engineer Cox and Gunner Thrasher—testified at the hearing. They all believed "heavy icing in the B-36's carburetors likely caused the engine problems that had led to the crash." The hearing did not address the fate of the atomic bomb because the presiding officer warned all witnesses that the flight's secret mission was strictly off-limits to the investigation. The other crew members were excused from testifying because they had no direct knowledge of the cause of the crash. The inquiry's secret report released years later concluded that the crew was competent, that the aircraft was in good mechanical condition and that icing of the carburetors was the cause of the crash.

The board recommended immediate corrective action to improve carburetors on the B-36 to ensure that they did not run excessively rich under normal power settings. Crews were better instructed in the importance and use of Aldis Lamps. Crews were to thoroughly familiarize themselves with procedures required to cope with carburetor, propeller and wing icing conditions. Briefings for future Alaskan maneuvers were to impress on all supervisory and flight crew personnel the severity of weather conditions that may be encountered in flight.

Years later, copilot Whitfield explained the board's findings:

> The carburetors in most aircraft are located aft of the engine. This arrangement permits warmed air from the engines to flow around the carburetors and will prevent all but throat icing. In the B-36, with the rearward facing engines, the carburetors were in front of the engines and thus constantly subjected to outside air temperatures. . . . In addition to this, the warm ocean currents that flow along the coast of B.C. cause heavy fog even in the coldest days of winter. This results in an abundance of moisture in the air above the coastline from which the ice would form. The constant rich mixtures soon caused a build-up of raw fuel in

the exhaust systems that eventually ignited, causing the fires.

A rumor circulated that crew members had been directly ordered not to talk to the press. If so it would have been a redundant order. According to Whitfield, "There was no briefing that I remember. Since we dealt with secret information routinely, we simply never talked to reporters about anything."

The board of inquiry filed its final report, and the air force prepared to move on. All evidence indicated the B-36 and its payload were lost but safely out of the reach of the Soviets. The air force and Convair addressed the problems with the carburetor icing on the B-36. Flight crews received more training on how to respond to the circumstances that had brought Ship 2075 down. As far as the air force was concerned, the case was closed.

On 3 September 1953, almost two and a half years after the crash, an unclassified message was received at USAF headquarters in Washington. It read: "B-36 aircraft located at 56 degrees 03 minutes north 128 degrees 23 minutes west at 6000-ft level. Plane has Eighth Air Force insignia. Number of plane on nose wheel door is 511. Believed to be aircraft missing since yr. 1950 enroute [from] Eielson [to] McChord." USAF brass in Washington greeted the message with astonishment. The only B-36 to ever go missing in the area was Ship 2075, and all evidence from the post-crash investigation indicated it was at the bottom of the Pacific Ocean. Nevertheless, a Royal Canadian Air Force (RCAF) flight reported sighting a B-36 on Mount Kologet, 60 miles east of Stewart, British Columbia, some 50 miles from the Alaska border. The message could not be ignored. The RCAF Lancaster that spotted the wreck was on an official search and rescue mission looking for American Ellis Hall. After a fishing trip to southeast Alaska, the millionaire was flying to the United States via Bellingham, Washington. The search found Ship 2075, but Ellis Hall and his airplane were never seen again.

The USAF hastily dispatched an investigation team. After all, the bomber was not supposed to be there—and yet it was. If the aircraft could show up where it wasn't supposed to be, what about the bomb? Had the crew covered up the fact that both a top-secret bomber and a

Remains of a demolished wing at the crash site of Ship 2075.
COURTESY DOUG DAVIDGE

nuclear weapon had not been destroyed but were lying in the mountains of northern British Columbia? More to the point, if an RCAF pilot could find the B-36 crash site just over 200 miles inland from the coast, so could the Soviets. The investigation team sent to the mountain town of Smithers, British Columbia, included Paul Gerhart, who had rigged the detonators to the Mark IV nuclear bomb on Ship 2075. The team was instructed to "destroy sensitive electronic equipment and search for the remains of missing crewmembers." The air force clearly held suspicions that linked weaponeer Ted Schreier's disappearance to the discovery of the B-36 in the British Columbia wilderness.

On 21 September 1953, a USAF service ground crew arrived in Smithers, British Columbia, which had been a RCAF airbase during World War II. Their mission was to take pictures of the B-36 wreck and to parachute supplies for a recovery team that would work its way up Mount Kologet. At Hazelton the recovery team hired local guides and packhorses to get them to the site. Late September in northern British Columbia is not known for its hiking weather. After nineteen days, the snow, cold and terrain defeated the recovery team. Returning to the United States, the team concluded that the plane would be safe for the winter. If the special operations team could not reach it, neither could the Soviets.

In early August 1954, a second USAF recovery team was back in Smithers. This time the team planned to use helicopters to reach the crash site. The first order of business was to find a secure location. Always vigilant about keeping the secrets of the Strategic Air Command safe, the team sought to operate away from prying eyes. A hangar shared by the British Columbia Forest Service and Skyway Air, a small charter airline, fit the bill perfectly. When the tenants were evicted from the hangar, they protested to the Canadian government. Their complaints fell on deaf ears. Did the Canadian government know a nuclear bomb might be on Canadian soil? Or was Canada simply cooperating unquestioningly with an ally? The answer is not known. Whatever the reason, the USAF received the full and immediate cooperation of the Canadian government.

The helicopters lifted off from the Smithers airport and quickly covered the distance to the crash site. The giant bomber was lying on its belly about a hundred feet below a saddle between two mountain peaks. While the bomber was certainly the worse for wear, it was mostly intact with the exception of the tail section. The flaps were up, the

Wreckage of Ship 2075. COURTESY DOUG DAVIDGE

main landing gear was retracted and the nose gear was facing the nose, indicating that the bomber had not been attempting to land at the time of the crash.

The team established a base camp near a small mountain lake approximately one-half mile from the crash site. Soon an airdrop delivered the equipment and explosives needed to reduce the top-secret bomber and its cargo to scrap metal. A Geiger counter was among the gear delivered to the special operations team. If the aircraft was in a place it was not supposed to be, the possibility existed, however remote, that the bomb was too. The Geiger counter was a precautionary measure.

Over the next ten days, the recovery team stripped the aircraft of its top-secret radar systems, bombsights and other sensitive electronic equipment. They then destroyed most exposed remains with high explosives and incendiary grenades. Except for the rear section, little was left untouched. Military explosives experts are nothing if not thorough, especially if they have lots of explosives to play with. The team worked with relish, destroying the forward section and engines. Their blasting threw the port wing and three engines across a small ridge 500 yards away. The demolition damaged many of the sensitive parts of the plane but did not completely destroy them. So the team tossed incendiary grenades into the fuselage to ignite the magnesium body. Fire completely destroyed the main landing gear, forward bomb bays and cockpit. The team left nothing identifiable of the forward structure. The rear section, including the vertical and horizontal stabilizers, remained on its back with its bomb bay doors facing the sky. Apparently, the demolition team was not worried that the Soviets could find anything of value there.

After completing the demolition, the members of the team loaded the equipment stripped from the B-36 into the helicopters, leaving behind barrels of unused explosives and the Geiger counter. They also abandoned their camp gear, including military rations, mess kits, bayonets and flashlights. Personal gear from Ship 2075's crew still littered the site, including military flight bags and luggage, Mae Wests, Goodrich survival suits and life rafts. It was simply impossible to airlift out any additional equipment or personal gear. As it was, the helicopters struggled to get airborne under the load of the recovery team and the salvaged items. Back in Smithers, a USAF transport plane was waiting to whisk the team and its secrets back to U.S. soil. Locals would report that the helicopters carried another burden from Mount Kologet. For years rumors circulated that the team had loaded a body bag into the waiting transport.

As extra insurance against the Soviets discovering what remained of the B-36, the team submitted its report with a false location, placing the crash site on Vancouver Island, hundreds of miles to the southwest.

In 1956 Doug Craig was a twenty-two-year-old civilian surveyor working out of Whitehorse, in the Yukon, on Operation Stikine, a program to update map information for the Geological Survey of Canada. On 23 June, working in a remote area near Smithers, he rediscovered the remains of Ship 2075. Scattered among the wreckage, he found a U.S. military parachute, the Geiger counter and its container, a canister of incendiary grenades and another canister of dynamite sticks.

Case containing the four spare detonators for the Fat Man bomb discovered in 1997. COURTESY DOUG DAVIDGE

Jim Roddick, who was working with Craig, recorded the find in his survey notebook:

> The wreck is located at El. 5500, Long. 128°34´, Lat. 56°05´. The aircraft was apparently on a westerly course when it struck within 100 ft or so of the ridge top. The fragments now visible are lower down the slope, probably thrown back by the explosion, or carried downhill by subsequent snow slides. The wreckage is concentrated in about a ¼ mile circular area, the upper part of which is covered by deep snow.
>
> There is considerable emergency gear, such as canned goods, clothing, etc., also armaments (incendiary grenades and 20 mm cannon shells). Although clothing is quite common, there is no indication of bodies. One fragment of a duffel bag has a name attached to it, H.L. Barry Captain AO-808341.

The survey team dutifully reported the find to the Royal Canadian Mounted Police (RCMP), expecting that a report of a downed American military aircraft, large quantities of explosives and 20 mm cannon shells would incite interest. Usually, the RCMP would take written statements, investigate the claim and open a file. But the RCMP did not react the way Craig expected. Instead, they listened to the story and did nothing. The survey team moved on, and the wreck gradually faded from memory, reduced to a few comments in field notes. But the location of Ship 2075 was now no longer a secret to the residents of Smithers. The site became a local attraction, and airplane parts, including the machine guns, found their way into local basements, garages and flea markets.

Forty-two years later, Doug Craig, now in retirement, had the luxury of time to explore the story of Ship 2075. Following extensive research into the crash and U.S. nuclear policy in the 1950s, he concluded that the remains of the Mark IV Fat Man bomb carried by Ship 2075 might still be at the crash site. He even speculated that the bomb's plutonium core might lay hidden among the remains on Mount Kologet. Either way, Craig worried that a potential nuclear hazard existed in the middle of British Columbia's pristine wilderness. Writing to the Environmental

Remains of Ship 2075 showing one of the escape hatches.
COURTESY DOUG DAVIDGE

Protection Branch of Environment Canada, Pacific and Yukon Region, and to the Canadian Department of National Defence (DND), Craig questioned the official version of the wreck. He wanted definitive answers about what had happened to the nuclear material aboard Ship 2075 and about whether the U.S. recovery team had removed a body back in 1954.

Both departments took Craig's concerns seriously, but they found a strange absence of official documentation about the incident. On 6 September 1996, the DND wrote that "based on information from Environment Canada, the body of one U.S. Air Force crewman had been found in the wreckage." The military was "reasonably certain the bomb was dropped over the Pacific and exploded." As to the plutonium core, a Canadian military memo dated nine months later concluded that, "It would make sense that the core would have traveled with the bomb, in case the weapon was needed in short order." Craig's concerns were not alleviated by the lack of definitive answers.

Craig's questions drew the attention of Doug Davidge, the manager of the Yukon Division of Environment Canada, who put pressure on the DND to conduct an environmental survey of the crash site to search for "radioactive contamination and other dangerous goods."

The DND agreed to set up a team, to provide air transportation, ground support, technical expertise and radiation detection equipment. On 11 August 1997, Craig, Davidge and Chris Thorp of DND's Ottawa headquarters, led by Lieutenant Commander David Knight, along with an aircrew, visited the B-36 crash site.

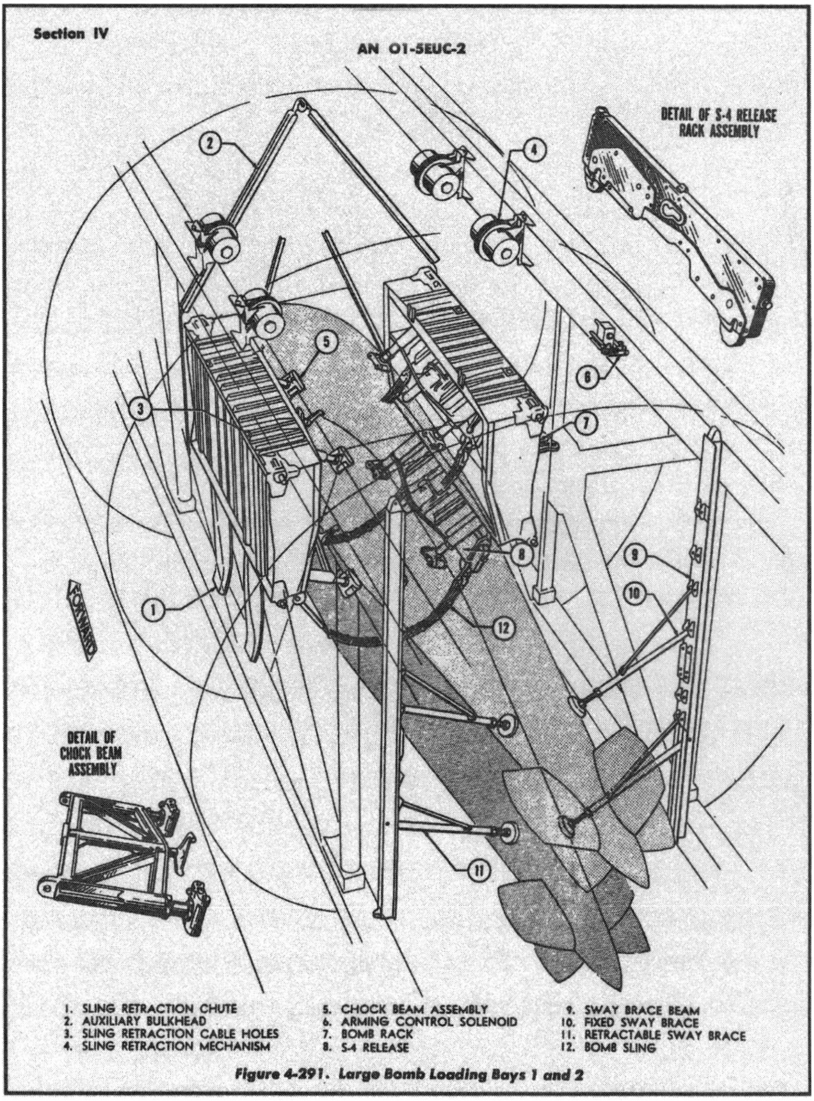

Figure 4-291. Large Bomb Loading Bays 1 and 2

B-36 bomb bay showing braces for securing the bomb in flight.

COURTESY USAF

After the helicopter settled into the saddle on Mount Kologet, Knight and Thorp ordered the others to stay aboard while they performed an initial survey of the site for radioactive contamination. When the preliminary results showed no elevated radiation levels, the others joined them. All survey team members were issued accumulative radiation detectors as an additional precaution. Over the next four days, they completed extensive radiation testing. They even tested sediment and vegetation, preserving the samples for later analysis by the DND. Ultimately, the DND concluded that "no high level radioactive material was found at the B-36 crash site on Mount Kologet. The aircraft electronics and gauges were the only radiation sources detected."

In the end the biggest concern identified by the DND team was not radiation but the explosives still on site. Knight reported that they found an aluminum box about the size of a small suitcase that contained the four spare detonators used on the Mark IV nuclear bomb. The team also found a 60- to 80-liter metal canister still filled with individual explosive charges. They also uncovered a small number of 20 mm cannon shells, small arms rounds and the barrels of high explosives left by the USAF crash-site investigation and demolition team.

On his return to Ottawa, Knight also reported to the British Columbia government that he had recovered a "number of personal items including leather flight hats with goggles, leather gloves, a cologne bottle, hair brush, a small souvenir totem pole . . . and an insignia pin from the 7th Bomb Wing with the motto 'Death From Above,' believed to belong to one of the surviving crew members of the 1950 B-36 . . . in the hope of finding their original owners." Based on the finds, the British Columbia government declared the crash site a historic site under provincial heritage legislation.

Two years later Doug Craig paid a third visit to the crash site. Joining him were Jim Roddick and Scott Deaver, a B-36 historian from Connecticut. Rounding out the expedition were Craig's son, Jason, and Dick Thrasher, who had been a gunner on Ship 2075 that night back in February 1950. According to Craig and Roddick, not much had changed since 1956. The scene brought back some painful memories for Dick Thrasher. Roddick reported:

> We rummaged through the now fully exposed wreckage. Only one large, intact piece of fuselage was present. It happened to contain the very hatch through which Dick Thrasher had exited from the left side of the rear compartment. It was very small. . . . He thinks, now, that the Mae West straps may have saved his life, because [they] delayed his pulling of the ripcord. Otherwise, he probably would have drifted into the water, as did Straley and Pollard, who jumped just before him.

Under a canopy of blue sky and bright sun, the group combed the rubble high on the ridge. Scott Deaver found what would be one of the most important artifacts to come from the wreckage of Ship 2075. From under a slab of talus, he pulled at an exposed piece of pipe. It turned out to be the missing birdcage that had been bolted to the wall of the B-36 on that stormy night forty-six years earlier. The birdcage contained the 8-inch lead-lined cylinder designed to hold the 13-pound plutonium core. Roddick believed other search teams failed to find the birdcage because it had been buried under the glacier that had receded over the years. The men dragged the heavy apparatus to the helicopter and rigged a suspension sling to fly it off the mountain. Roddick would write later that, "We were a bit worried that the helicopter pilot would question us about our odd-looking freight, but he was in a hurry and wasn't curious."

Deaver contracted a carpenter in Stewart to build a box to transport the find back to the United States. The men attempted to load the large, heavy box into the car but found it was too big for the trunk. After some thought, they pushed it into the backseat, and Dick Thrasher wedged into the space left over for the ride back to Terrace. From Terrace, Deaver and the birdcage flew to Vancouver and then across the Canada–United States border. Deaver was concerned he might have trouble crossing an international border with his strange souvenir, but after a few tense moments explaining to a bored customs agent that the "piece of plane wreckage was destined for a museum," the box and Deaver were on their way to Connecticut.

When Deaver was safely home, he opened the lead-lined container and found it "gleaming and pristine inside, but empty." The air force had been telling the truth. There had been an atomic bomb aboard Ship 2075, but the nuclear core had never left the watchful eyes of the Atomic Energy Commission.

Deaver did not keep the birdcage. When another researcher mentioned to the U.S. National Atomic Museum that Deaver had a birdcage, they contacted him. First and foremost a historian, Deaver agreed to turn it over to the museum.

In 2004 Canadian filmmaker Mike Jorgenson and Canadian nuclear weapons expert Dr. John Clearwater teamed up to film a documentary about the flight of Ship 2075. Clearwater had worked as an analyst and historian for Air Command Headquarters at Canadian Forces Base Winnipeg until he left to write *The Birth of Strategic Arms Control in the Johnson Administration, 1963–1969*, *Canadian Nuclear Weapons* and *U.S. Nuclear Weapons in Canada.*

At the crash site, Clearwater found further evidence that a Mark IV nuclear bomb had been aboard Ship 2075 but no evidence that the aircraft had been carrying a second atomic bomb. A rumor about a possible second bomb had circulated in the aviation community for years. Among the wreckage, he identified four sway braces, the H-frame that supported the bomb shackle, one of the giant chain hoists used to lift the Mark IV into the forward bomb bay and the bomb shackle that steadied the Mark IV in flight. Writing in his expedition journal, he reported that after exhaustive analysis he had absolute proof that a second nuclear bomb had not been loaded aboard the B-36:

> As for a second bomb, bomb bays Number 2 and Number 3 carried giant fuel cells to extend the range of the aircraft. These were hung from the major bomb racks, just like the Grand Slam bomb. The rear bomb bay was equipped with regular bomb racks outfitted for conventional bombing with standard high explosive ordinance and survival kits.

Clearwater continued his search for artifacts and noted "a vast amount of personal gear strewn downhill of the bomb bays." This gear included survival equipment (one-man life rafts, an immersion suit, a large white silk parachute and survival kits), personal clothing and toiletries, and finally a rank insignia believed to belong to Lieutenant Colonel MacDonald, the observer on Ship 2075.

After five days of investigation, the film crew left the crash site for the last time. The wreck of Ship 2075 had finally given up the last of its secrets.

CHAPTER EIGHT

Controversy and Conspiracy

In 1950 the crash of Ship 2075 generated controversy among military and civilian agencies. The flagship of America's defense strategy against Soviet expansionism had gone missing and with it a Fat Man atomic bomb. The Atomic Energy Commission (AEC) wanted to know the fate of its bomb. The air force wanted to be certain its bomber's top-secret systems could not fall into Soviet hands. Legislators in Washington wanted answers to questions about the reliability of the B-36 bomber. When the crash site of Ship 2075 was discovered on Mount Kologet three years after the crash, the questions and concerns multiplied. If the bomber, for reasons unknown, had come down hundreds of miles from its presumed location at the bottom of the Pacific Ocean, what other presumptions could be equally wrong?

Over the years, conspiracy theories began to swirl around the mission of Ship 2075. Did the B-36 crash on Canadian soil with a nuclear bomb aboard, or was the bomb jettisoned over Canadian waters? Was the plutonium core aboard, and was it yet to be found on Mount Kologet? Was the bomber carrying a second atomic bomb? Did Ted Schreier bail out, only to be lost at sea? If so, how did Ship 2075 make it hundreds of miles northeast of its presumed location in the Pacific? Or did Schreier take the controls and attempt to fly the crippled bomber back to base in Alaska? Why did the air force continue to shroud the flight in such secrecy? Conspiracy theorists have pulled together single threads of the story in an attempt to make whole cloth out of speculation. Looking back with contemporary eyes to events over fifty years in the past, some succumb to the temptation to weave conjecture about American foreign policy in the 1950s, reckless military behavior and cloak-and-dagger dissembling into a new narrative of Ship 2075's mission. Such interpretations stretch the boundaries between possibility and plausibility.

For the aircrews of the Strategic Air Command (SAC), their commanders and the politicians who approved the B-36 program, the United States of the 1950s was entrenched in a battle against Communism. Virtually everyday, newspapers carried accounts of Soviet aggression in Europe. The men of SAC believed in their hearts they were protecting the United States and the free world from the threat of Communism. Their actions cannot be judged outside the context of their times nor can they be separated from the depth of their convictions. As they took to the skies for their marathon, maximum-effort training flights with the Fat Man tucked in the bomb bay, they were preparing for a nuclear war they assumed to be inevitable. They reasoned that their presence in the skies was the very thing keeping war at bay, at least for the moment. The rules of war applied to their motives and decisions.

As with the details of any top-secret military program, some questions about the mission of Ship 2075 may never be answered. In an age before closed-circuit cameras, digital recording, flight data recorders and computers, accident investigation was much more an art than a science. Investigators depended on eyewitness testimony to understand the story. According to Andrew Roberts, an evidence expert at Leeds University, the courts have long recognized that eyewitness identification evidence is "inherently unreliable." So it is with the story of Ship 2075. Despite the fact that the men involved in the 13 February 1950 mission of Ship 2075 were trained airmen and skilled observers, their accounts vary. The official inquiry contained dozens of inconsistencies in the crew members' testimonies, sometimes on key issues. For example, both the pilot and the engineering officer of the ferry crew reported that problems with Ship 2075 were not serious. Commander Barry, however, testified that the bomber had serious mechanical difficulties on takeoff. Barry also testified that he had not been formally briefed that he could deviate from Ship 2075's mission plan if severe icing conditions occurred. But under oath his commanding officer swore such a briefing had been given.

Forensic psychologist Dr. Fiona Gabbert of Aberdeen University studies the distortions in eyewitness recollection. "Memories are very vulnerable to error," she concludes. "If you witness a crime and then read a local news report, everything can be combined in your memory at a later date. It can be hard to distinguish between what you saw and another source of information." None of the inconsistencies in the eyewitness accounts about the loss of Ship 2075 are unusual for those caught in the throes of disaster.

The conspiracy theorists suffer from a selective perspective. They focus their interpretations on frequently uncorroborated eyewitness testimony that supports their cause and dismiss accounts that do not. For example, conspiracy theories maintaining the presence of a second nuclear bomb aboard Ship 2075 dwell on the takeoff from Eielson Air Force Base. Commander Barry testified that it was a heavy takeoff requiring maximum stick. Some have speculated that the weight of a second nuclear weapon accounted for the difficulty in getting airborne. Nevertheless, the overwhelming weight of evidence indicates there was no second bomb aboard Ship 2075. Despite the fact that many details about the Fat Man bomb remain classified, the Historical Records Agency of the United States Air Force has released the loading manifest for Ship 2075. It confirms that a single 10,000-pound atomic bomb was loaded in the forward bomb bay of the B-36 on that wintry afternoon at Eielson AFB. The weapon was the Mark IV Fat Man, a slightly modified version of the one dropped on Nagasaki in 1945. In 1987 a U.S. military report listing nuclear weapons accidents acknowledged that the British Columbia incident was the first to involve a missing nuclear bomb. If the U.S. government has already admitted to a nuclear bomb aboard Ship 2075, it has little reason not to admit to a second.

Though much of the official documentation about the crash remains confidential to this day, those who have examined the crash site and who have gone on record agree that the 1954 special operations recovery and demolition team was especially thorough. The team destroyed the sections of the giant bomber that contained its most closely guarded secrets. The recovery team obliterated the forward bomb bay, which held the Mark IV, but they left the rear bomb bay essentially intact. If aboard, a second nuclear bomb would have been carried in the rear bomb bay because the center bomb bays contained extra fuel tanks. If a second bomb had been in the rear, the special operations team would undoubtedly have destroyed that section of the bomber as well. Certainly, they were not short of the means to do so for they left a large amount of explosives on the mountainside.

Further, Dr. John Clearwater's extensive examination of the rear bomb bay in 2004 concluded that it "was equipped with regular bomb racks." If there had been a second 10,000-pound nuclear bomb, it would have required the heavy lifting gear that Clearwater found in the remains of the forward bomb bay, where the known bomb was located. Finally, the investigation by the Canadian Department of National Defense (DND) in 1997 found no indication of elevated radiation levels at the crash site. If a second bomb had gone down with the Ship 2075, it would certainly have heavily contaminated the area.

The preponderance of evidence confirms that Ship 2075's difficulty in getting aloft resulted from mechanical difficulties coupled with ice on the fuselage and wings. Commander Barry was concerned that the aircraft did not receive the required maintenance on the ground at Eielson AFB because of the short turnaround conducted under extreme weather conditions. At the official inquiry, testimony confirmed a number of these problems. As the bomber headed onto the runway, the turbo-assisted boost on engine number five was not working, and engine number one was not able to deliver full power. A thin layer of ice covered the airfoils of the bomber, and water possibly contaminated the fuel. In the atmosphere of heightened anxieties that prevailed in February 1950, however, commanders and crews tolerated more risk and lower safety standards. Ship 2075 received clearance for takeoff.

Conspiracy theorists also have speculated that Fat Man's plutonium core was aboard Ship 2075. Some make much of General LeMay's credo that training was to be "as close to war as it gets." Nevertheless, considerable evidence indicates that Ship 2075 did not carry the Fat Man's plutonium core. SAC conducted training missions with a lead dummy core to mitigate danger in the event of an accident. The first instance of the Air Force possessing atomic bombs armed with plutonium cores did not occur until April 1951, when President Truman assigned nine Mark IV atomic bombs to the custody of General Hoyt Vandenberg, USAF Chief of Staff.

Strict operating procedures governed the handling of a plutonium core aboard a B-36. The core was to be secured in the birdcage that was bolted to the bulkhead in the bomb bay. In the event of an order for a nuclear attack, the weaponeer was to transfer the core to the bomb. If the aircraft faced imminent disaster, the birdcage with its plutonium core was to be jettisoned for recovery or strapped to the bomb and destroyed with it. Surviving crew members of Ship 2075 have publicly acknowledged that the bomb was aboard but that the bomber carried only a dummy lead core. In an interview years after the crash, copilot Whitfield confirmed that the core was a dummy and that, furthermore, the equipment required to transfer the core from the birdcage to the bomb was not aboard the bomber. The fact that the crew of Ship 2075 did not follow standard operating procedures in jettisoning the birdcage with the bomb supports the conclusion that it did not contain a plutonium core. Additionally, the 1954 recovery team sent to the crash site would have easily located the highly radioactive core with their Geiger counter if it had existed. They certainly would have salvaged it intact in the birdcage. Some theorists contend the recovery team removed the plutonium core and transferred it to another container. But such handling of nuclear material seems unlikely at best and would have been a dangerous waste of effort. It is also highly doubtful that the recovery team would have left a classified piece of equipment like the birdcage lying on the mountainside. When the birdcage was eventually discovered at the crash site, its interior was in pristine condition, and independent tests confirmed no lingering radiation in the birdcage. It had never housed the plutonium core.

Investigation by the Canadian DND team of the crash site in 1997 provided final and compelling evidence that a second bomb or a plutonium core was not aboard Ship 2075. Asked in an interview if there was evidence of a second bomb or a plutonium core, investigator Chris Thorp responded, "We went there to prove whether it was still, in fact, on site, and everything we accounted for definitely seems to indicate that there was nothing not explainable on that site." Had the core been among the wreckage of Ship 2075? "Our indications say 'No,'" Thorpe reported.

Others, taking the theory a generous step forward, have contended that the crew of Ship 2075 never jettisoned the single Mark IV bomb aboard Ship 2075. They claim that crews on fishing boats heard the sound of a B-36 flying low overhead but not the detonation of the conventional high explosives that destroyed the bomb over the water. Canadian aviation researcher and co-founder of the Broken Arrow Aircraft Society in Terrace, British Columbia, Carl Healey, contends "that there were no reports of loud explosions that night in the Princess Royal Island area." He believes that if the aircrew had detonated the Mark IV, "the sound would have been deafening."

However, both the flight path of the B-36 and the weather conditions on the night of 13–14 February 1950 can account for the failure of the fishing crews to hear or recall hearing the explosion. At 40,000 feet the engines of the B-36 rattled windows. At 8,000 feet the giant aircraft was even louder. It would have been almost impossible to hear anything over the sound of the engines. Furthermore, gale-force winds buffeted the boats. Hunkered below decks, the fishing crews rode out the storm. The continuous roar of the B-36 would certainly impress itself on the fishermen's memories, but the sound of the exploding bomb, if heard, would be largely indistinguishable from the sounds of the storm rocking the boats. A muffled bang on a fishing boat in a gale would not have stood out in the crews' memories.

A variation on the theory that the bomb was not destroyed proposes that the aircrew jettisoned it but that it did not detonate. According to this scenario, the Fat Man rests (and rusts) unexploded and undetected at the bottom of Queen Charlotte Sound. However, this theory is in direct opposition to statements by the crew of Ship 2075. Gerhart, Thrasher and Whitfield all claim that they either saw or felt the bomb explode.

Finally, some conspiracy theorists believe that the continuing secrecy surrounding the crash of Ship 2075 is evidence that the U.S. government is still hiding some terrible truth. But the real truth is a pedestrian one. In 1950 the B-36 and the Fat Man were America's most closely guarded secret weapons. SAC, its aircraft, its men and their missions constituted the frontline of defense and deterrence against Soviet aggression and expansionism. The American government necessarily needed to protect its military secrets.

The board of inquiry into the crash of Ship 2075 called a large number of witnesses. But the presiding officer quickly established the ground rules. Even though the inquiry itself was classified, it would allow no discussion of the top-secret details of the mission. The board's sole object was to determine the cause of the crash. The atomic bomb was not to be mentioned. Barry, Cox and Thrasher testified about their actions on the night of 13–14 February because those three had most direct knowledge about the operation and airworthiness of Ship 2075. The other crew members were excused. Those who testified believed the report would remain sealed forever. They had every reason to be completely candid. While the report was eventually released and is now widely available, the witnesses could not have predicted this in 1950. Further, they were the warriors of SAC, dedicated to an ideal of honor and patriotism that may appear outmoded to modern eyes. The likelihood of the men of Ship 2075 dissembling about their actions on an official mission is remote.

Some conspiracy theorists raise questions about the documentation the USAF has released—and what it has not. They call attention, for example, to the fact that on "some government reports the U.S. Air Force still lists the crash site as on Vancouver Island, [while] other documents give the wrong latitude and longitude of the wreckage. The 1954 report on the recovery mission can't be found and about 100 pages of the report on the original crash are still classified top-secret." In spite of these claims, the official accident report clearly identifies Princess Royal Island as the bailout point and provides other details about the bomber's direction, speed and altitude. Details about the location of the crash, including both a general description and specific longitude and latitude, are also contained in the report. A slight discrepancy exists between the coordinates recorded in 1953 and those taken with modern GPS systems, but the original coordinates are within walking distance of the actual crash site.

In order for the board to fully understand the mission of Ship 2075, it must have documented the bomber's payload. Such documentation may account for the still-classified pages of the inquiry report, and its absence is entirely consistent with U.S. military policy concerning disclosing details about atomic weapons. The United States still considers the Mark IV top secret—and for good reason in an age that resonates with concern over rogue states developing nuclear weapon technology. To this day, the design and construction details of the bomb are deleted from official documents. As to the missing 1954 report on the recovery operation at the crash site, the U.S. military lost many reports when they microfilmed millions of documents in the late 1950s.

Other conspiracy theories probe the differences between the manner in which the USAF managed the crash site of Ship 2075 and the sites of other B-36 crashes in Canada. The 1954 team largely destroyed Ship 2075. The same treatment did not apply to later mishaps with B-36s in Canada, one on 12 February 1953 near Goose Bay, Labrador, and another just over a month later near Burgoynes Cove, Newfoundland. But the crash of Ship 2075 was different in a number of significant ways. No evidence exists to indicate that a nuclear weapon was aboard either of the bombers that crashed in 1953. Both crashes on Canada's east coast were more likely out of the reach of Soviet agents, and, in any event, by 1953 the technology aboard the B-36 was no longer cutting edge, no longer as valuable for the Soviets to discover and no longer as valuable for the USAF to protect.

Finally, conspiracy theorists point to the continuing secrecy of living crew members, who have never spoken openly about a number of events on that February night in 1950. Some conspiracy theorists believe they were threatened into silence. However, threats were not required to keep their silence. Patriotism, duty and honor ensured it. By the choice of their profession, military elites around the world aspire to be different, whether they are the Special Air Service, the Canadian Airborne, Navy Seals or the Strategic Air Command. For them, loyalty to their mission and the members of their unit is an unquestioned principle of behavior. According to Dr. John Clearwater,

> U.S. secrecy about the site itself was not due to the presence of an atomic bomb, it was due to the fact that the aircraft itself contained many secrets of the early nuclear age. The bombsight and various nuclear weapons tools for the bomb-armorer were considered far too sensitive to leave for anyone to find. The USAF also feared that certain records of the training operation itself would have survived, and this would reveal U.S. nuclear war plans.

The true significance of the crash of Ship 2075 resides in it being the first to involve the loss of a nuclear weapon. Over foreign waters, the United States Air Force detonated the world's first so-called dirty bomb. The story, now relegated to history and replaced by the War on Terror, with its fears of dirty bombs and a new era of nuclear weapons proliferation, does not need conspiracy theories to make it compelling. The story provides insight into the global politics and military culture of America in the 1950s. It is a tale of the heightened fears stirred by the Cold War and the earliest days of the nuclear brinkmanship that would ignite the nuclear arms race. It is a story of people and technology, of passion and patriotism, of daring and heroism.

At the heart of the story Ship 2075's last training mission is one remaining controversy: How did Ship 2075 arrive at its final resting place high on a windswept ridge of British Columbia's Skeena Mountains? Jim Roddick, who was on the team that discovered the B-36 wreckage in 1956, speculates that the strong southeast wind blew the unpiloted circling B-36 to Mount Kologet. He argues that the gale acted like a river that carried the bomber in its current for approximately three hours. Reduction of the fuel load, possible carburetor de-icing due to drier inland conditions and engines running at full throttle allowed the aircraft to climb above the intervening terrain, much of which is considerably higher than the 5,000-foot altitude at which the crew bailed out.

This theory has its supporters. However, the testimony of Commander Barry and two other crew members at the official hearing contradicted this supposition. He specifically stated that the bomber changed direction from clockwise to counterclockwise. Under a fully deployed parachute canopy from 5,000 feet, Barry's jump would have lasted about five minutes. If Ship 2075 continued in its clockwise turn and returned over the men, it would have had to have flown a full circle in less than that time. Flying at the reported air speed of 155 mph, the maximum circumference the bomber could have traced in its flight would have been less than 13 miles with a diameter of 4 miles. This is a tight turn for a bomber as large as the B-36, not a gentle curve as Barry described. Even under full power, it is difficult to turn a modern Boeing 747 so sharply. Further, each tight turn would cause Ship 2075 to lose altitude, corkscrewing it into the ocean unless additional power was applied. Even if the drier overland conditions alleviated carburetor icing, the drag caused by the turn would have prevented the altitude gains needed to clear the terrain between Princess Royal Island and Mount Kologet. On continuous high power in a continuous turn, the giant bomber would have descended, not climbed. Such a descent was Commander Barry's original intention.

The most compelling argument for how ship 2075 crashed on Mount Kologet is that Captain Ted Schreier flew it there. Though eyewitnesses claimed that a body bag was loaded onto an airplane by the recovery team when they returned from the crash site in 1954, the USAF has never admitted to recovering a body on the mountain. It is feasible that the recovery team left a good deal of equipment, including the Geiger counter and explosives, because they needed to lighten the load on the helicopters to make room for the weight of Schreier's body. Jim Roddick found no human remains on Mount Kologet when he discovered the crash site in 1956, and none were later discovered by local looters, by the Canadian Department of National Defence investigation team or by the documentary film crew who combed the site.

Jefferson Barracks National Cemetery in St. Louis, Missouri, records Captain Theodore F. Schreier's death as 14 February 1950 and his official burial on 17 July 1952. His gravesite is shared with the four other unrecovered crew members of Ship 2075. A spokesman for Jefferson Barracks explained that is common "when the bodies are either not recovered or unidentifiable, to bury or list the dead in the same grave." If Schreier's body was recovered in 1954, his final resting place remains a mystery.

Wherever the location of Theodore Schreier's remains, one can imagine his last hours. Alone on the B-36, he recognizes his career at SAC may be in ruins. As the weaponeer responsible for a Fat Man bomb, he assumes responsibility for its loss. As he tries to rig his parachute correctly, he realizes he will bail out over the frigid winter waters of the Pacific with little hope of survival. He decides on another course of action and hauls himself up the steps to the flight deck of the B-36. Seizing the controls, Schreier reverses the giant aircraft's course.

Gale force winds rock the airframe. The ailing engines trail streams of sparks. Flying at first blind through fog and cloud, and then through the gray and black of a moonless northern night, he charts a course for home and safety. With only a compass and dead reckoning as his navigation guides, relying on the skills and guts forged in combat, he comes within a few minutes, a few miles and a few feet of single-handedly protecting one of America's military secrets.

At Carswell Air Force Base, four of the five who died aboard Ship 2075 have streets named in their honor. Ted Schreier did not receive the same distinction. SAC, especially as led by the unforgiving Curtis LeMay, presumably did not honor the memory of an officer who had disobeyed operational procedures and left America's top-secret bomber potentially within reach of the Soviets. Captain Ted Schreier's final motives and moments cannot be known with certainty. He would never have described himself as a hero. If anything, Ted Schreier is distinguished by his ordinariness in extraordinary times. He would have seen himself simply as a pilot doing his job to defend his country with the utmost of his courage, talent and training. Yet, by any standard, Schreier was a hero. He did what his country asked of him—and more—however quaint and archaic the intervening post-Watergate, post–Iran-Contra years may make such an answering of the call of duty appear. The time has long past for the United States Air Force to acknowledge the true fate of Ted Schreier and to honor his memory in the manner it justly deserves. The final chapter in the story of Ship 2075 will be written when a street named Schreier takes its place on the map of Carswell Air Force Base, Texas.

NOTES

CHAPTER ONE NOTES

p. 6, *"help end the war in the Pacific"* / "United States Considered Using Atomic Bomb in Europe: Tibbets."

p. 6, *"cause Japan to surrender"* / "What Have We Done?"

p. 7, *"B-29s were actually spotted"* / Manhattan Engineer District.

p. 7, *"effects of radiation"* / "Damage Caused by Atomic Bombs."

p. 8, *"countries after the war ended"* / "Cold War 1945–1990."

p. 9, *"25 million, mostly civilians"* / *Ibid.*

p. 9, *"land war in Europe"* / *Ibid.*

p. 10, *"amounts of* nuclear *material"* / "Civilian Control of Atomic Energy (1945–1946)."

p. 10, *"Atomic Energy Act of 1946"* / *Ibid.*

p. 10, *"then in the Army's possession"* / *Ibid.*

p. 10, *"in the interest of national defense"* / *Ibid.*

p. 10, *"midnight, 31 December 1946"* / *Ibid.*

p. 10, *"turned out to hear the great orator"* / "Winston Churchill's Iron Curtain Speech."

p. 12, *"Cold War in the public's perception."* / *Ibid.*

p. 12, *"Soviet espionage activities in the West"* / Butler, Don. "Gouzenko affair."

p. 12, *"trade for freedom in the West"* / *Ibid.*

p. 12, *"door to his freedom"* / *Ibid.*

p. 12, *"looking for the missing spy documents"* / *Ibid.*

p. 13, *"the Communist Party's national organizer in Canada"* / Jonas, George. "The Secret Garden."

p. 13, *"Julius and Ethel Rosenberg were exposed and arrested" / Ibid.*

p. 13, *"new identities by the Canadian government" / Ibid.*

p. 13, *"Only in the will of mankind lies the answer"* / "Baruch Plan."

p. 13, *"implementation of atomic energy and its uses" / Ibid.*

p. 15, *"our own methods and conceptions of human society"* / "Kennan's Long Telegram."

p. 15, *"armed minorities or by outside pressures"* / "Harry Truman and the Truman Doctrine."

p. 15, *"ended its longstanding policy of isolationism" / Ibid.*

p. 16, *"counter strong Communist movements"* / "Truman Doctrine Speech."

p. 16, *"George Marshall, the United States Secretary of State" / Ibid.*

p. 16, *"enjoy unprecedented growth and prosperity"* / De Long, Bradford, and Barry Eichengreen. "The Marshall Plan."

p. 16, *"Europe along the path toward continental integration" / Ibid.*

p. 17, *"Moscow-friendly government"* / "Czechoslovakia Coup of 1948."

p. 17, *"the Soviets, became a potent military force" / Ibid.*

p. 17, *"goal of 250,000 within a year" / Ibid.*

p. 17, *"Chinese Civil War that had been underway since 1946"* / Ah Xiang. "Chinese Civil Wars."

p. 17, *"defend against a communist advance, from the United States" / Ibid.*

p. 17, *"begin the final push against the Nationalists" / Ibid.*

p. 18, *"People's Liberation Army rolled south" / Ibid.*

p. 18, *"linked Britain, France and the Benelux countries"* / NATO. "1948."

p. 18, "to consider an armed attack against any one of them as an attack against all" / NATO. "The North Atlantic Treaty."

p. 18, *"Supreme Commander of NATO military forces"* / Peluso, Tony. "The Formation of NATO."

p. 19, *"the war continued with Nazi Germany"* / "Rise of the Nuclear Age."

p. 19, *"Secrecy was paramount"* / *Ibid.*

p. 19, *"both the United States and Great Britain"* / *Ibid.*

p. 19, *"virtual replica of the U.S. Fat Man bomb"* / *Ibid.*

p. 19, *"the Soviet Union would not have the bomb within five years"* / Steury, Donald P. "How the CIA Missed Stalin's Bomb."

p. 19, *"arrested on 2 February 1950"* / Tweedie, Neil and Peter Day. "Arrogance of the atom spy."

p. 19, *"he earned his PhD in physics"* / "Klaus Fuchs (1911–1988)."

p. 20, *"hired to work on the British atomic bomb project"* / *Ibid.*

p. 20, *"was working on in secret"* / *Ibid.*

p. 20, *"promptly signed the Official Secrets Act"* / *Ibid.*

p. 20, *"first operational test of a nuclear weapon"* / *Ibid.*

p. 21, *"Eniwetok Atoll of uranium and plutonium bombs"* / Myers, Peter. "Pavel Sudoplatov, Special Tasks."

p. 21, *"twenty kilos of plutonium per month"* / *Ibid.*

p. 21, *"avoided prison had he not volunteered his confession"* / Tweedie, Neil, and Peter Day. "Arrogance of the atom spy."

p. 21, *"East Germany to work on their nuclear program"* / *Ibid.*

p. 21, *"end of the 1940s or even into the early 1950s"* / Myers, Peter. "Pavel Sudoplatov, Special Tasks."

CHAPTER TWO NOTES

p. 24, *"delivered by long-range bombers based in the United States"* / Ford, Daniel. "B-36: Bomber at the Crossroads."

p. 24, *"that will preclude outright military assault."* / Kunsman, David M., and Douglas B. Lawson. *A Primer on U.S. Strategic Nuclear Policy*: p. 9.

p. 24, *"deterrence became 'a façade.'"* / *Ibid.*, p. 9.

p. 24, *"attack against NATO by the Soviet Union and its allies"* / *Ibid.*, p. 10.

p. 24, *"thereby deny him achievement of his objectives"* / *Ibid.*, p. 12.

p. 25, *"bombing attacks against the Communists"* / *Ibid.*, p. 22.

p. 25, "*war-related facilities in major cities*" / *Ibid.*, p. 22.

p. 25, "*in the event of war is to be made by the Chief Executive*" / *Ibid.*, p. 23.

p. 25, "*bombing by 133 nuclear weapons*" / *Ibid.*, p. 23.

p. 25, "*power of the Soviet leadership to dominate the people*" / *Ibid.*, p. 23.

p. 26, "*attack by itself would not defeat the Soviet Union*" / *Ibid.*, p. 23.

p. 26, "*admitted that war with the Soviets was considered almost inevitable*" / *Ibid.*, p. 26.

p. 26, "*well beyond the range of any existing bomber*" / Wachsmuth, Wayne. *B-36 Peacemaker*: p. 3.

p. 26, "*Boeing Aircraft Company, responded*" / "Weapons of mass destruction (WMD). B-36 Peacemaker."

p. 27, "*the mainstay of the U.S. World War II arsenal*" / *Ibid.*

p. 28, "*on human resources and materials caused by the war*" / *Ibid.*

p. 28, "*its success in delivering the B-24 Liberator*" / *Ibid.*

p. 28, "'*entangled with red tape' and 'constantly changing directives*'" / *Ibid.*

p. 28, "*new aircraft was redesignated the B-36*" / *Ibid.*

p. 29, "*Liberators were flying missions around the world*" / Ford, Daniel. "B-36: Bomber at the Crossroads."

p. 29, "*capable of reaching Japan from there*" / *Ibid.*

p. 30, "*redesigned, adding more than another ton*" / "Weapons of mass destruction (WMD). B-36 Peacemaker."

p. 30, "*weight from increasing another 3,500 pounds*" / *Ibid.*

p. 30, "*rearrangement of the forward crew compartment*" / *Ibid.*

p. 30, "*just three air bases in the entire United States*" / *Ibid.*

p. 30, "*even reduced weight by 1,500 pounds*" / *Ibid.*

p. 30, "*ready when the army arrived for its inspection*" / *Ibid.*

p. 30, "*reductions in both armament and crew size*" / *Ibid.*

p. 30, "*divert scarce resources to the experimental project*" / *Ibid.*

p. 30, "*mired in its own production problems*" / *Ibid.*

p. 30, *"going to give them up without a fight"* / *Ibid.*

p. 30, *"the queue of priorities yet again"* / *Ibid.*

p. 31, *"essential wind tunnel tests on the B-36 until spring 1944"* / *Ibid.*

p. 31, *"same time wasted scarce resources"* / *Ibid.*

p. 31, *"and increase the costs by $61 million"* / *Ibid.*

p. 31, *"lower the tail enough to provide clearance"* / Ford, Daniel. "B-36: Bomber at the Crossroads."

p. 32, *"operate in terms of cost per ton per mile"* / "Weapons of mass destruction (WMD). B-36 Peacemaker."

p. 32, *"'placeholder' engines for the test flight"* / "Convair B-36."

p. 32, *"particularly in the shape of the airfoil"* / "Weapons of mass destruction (WMD). B-36 Peacemaker."

p. 32, *"The B-36 was grounded again"* / *Ibid.*

p. 33, *"who took the greatest umbrage"* / Ford, Daniel. "B-36: Bomber at the Crossroads."

p. 33, *"diminishing defense budget should go to them"* / *Ibid.*

p. 33, *"admirals went to war in Washington"* / *Ibid.*

p. 33, *"bomb to be delivered from Maine to Leningrad"* / *Ibid.*

p. 33, *"weapons, and that was far from certain"* / *Ibid.*

p. 34, *"they would be within range of the Soviet Union"* / *Ibid.*

p. 34, *"first production B-36A ready to fly before the prototype"* / Jenkins, Dennis R. *Convair B-36 Peacemaker*: p. 33.

p. 34, *"fleets of fighter aircraft or nuclear bombers"* / *Ibid.* p. 40.

p. 35, *"bombs on target from 25,000 feet"* / "7th Bombardment Wing Operations, Carswell AFB, 1946–1948."

p. 35, *"built by Consolidated Vultee Aircraft Corporation"* / *Ibid.*

p. 37, *"with a service ceiling of 42,500 feet"* / Ford, Daniel. "B-36: Bomber at the Crossroads."

p. 37, *"only met but exceeded the original 1941 requirements"* / Baugher, Joe. "Convair B-36B Peacemaker."

p. 37, *"they were back in their beds"* / *Ibid.*

p. 38, *"nuclear weapons to the heart of the Soviet Union"* / Ford, Daniel. "B-36: Bomber at the Crossroads."

p. 38, *"roared over the Capitol building in Washington, D.C."* / *Ibid.*

p. 38, *"president personally inspected the new bombers"* / Baugher, Joe. "Convair B-36B Peacemaker."

p. 38, *"unleashed the famed 'Revolt of the Admirals'"* / Ford, Daniel. "B-36: Bomber at the Crossroads."

p. 39, *"$6.5 million to various Democratic politicians"* / *Ibid.*

p. 39, *"by at least three of the U.S. Navy's own fighters"* / *Ibid.*

p. 39, *"very limited maneuverability"* / *Ibid.*

p. 39, *"Stuart Symington, the civilian head of the air force"* / *Ibid.*

p. 39, *"return non-stop to the point of takeoff"* / *Ibid.*

p. 40, *"'I think I was wrong,'"* / *Ibid.*

p. 40, *"procurement of the B-36 bomber,' the committee concluded"* / *Ibid.*

p. 40, *"two pressurized crew cabins separated by bomb bays"* / *Ibid.*

p. 40, *"comfortably fit under one wing of the giant B-36"* / *Ibid.*

p. 40, *"landing gear in flight"* / *Ibid.*

p. 41, *"observe the exterior condition of the aircraft"* / Baugher, Joe. "Convair B-36B Peacemaker."

p. 41, *"most powerful and sophisticated piston aircraft engines ever built"* / *Ibid.*

p. 41, *"R-4360-41 engines with fluid injection"* / *Ibid.*

p. 41, *"shorter runways and delivered better overall performance"* / *Ibid.*

p. 41, *"unburned fuel in the exhaust caught fire"* / "B36 Pacemaker: Big, Bad and Beautiful."

p. 41, *"often caused the remaining engines to fail"* / *Ibid.*

p. 44, *"the B-36's six engines rattled windows on the ground"* / Ford, Daniel. "B-36: Bomber at the Crossroads."

p. 44, *"The plane's giant 19-foot propellers"* / Jenkins, Dennis R. *Convair B-36 Peacemaker*: p. 9.

p. 44, *"You looked up into the sky to try to find this thing, and it was just a tiny cross, it was so high"* / Ford, Daniel. "B-36: Bomber at the Crossroads."

p. 44, *"three forward gunners and five rear gunners"* / Baugher, Joe. "Convair B-36B Peacemaker."

p. 45, *"had to move his forward and vice versa"* / Morris, Ted A. "Flying the Aluminum and Magnesium Overcast."

p. 45, *"crew had to wear heavy winter clothing, even in summer" / Ibid.*

p. 45, *"onto the crew on the flight deck" / Ibid.*

p. 45, *"stay near the controls of the massive bomber" / Ibid.*

p. 46, *"also led to the rear gun turret"* / Ford, Daniel. "B-36: Bomber at the Crossroads."

p. 46, *"transport hot meals from the galley in the rear of the plane" / Ibid.*

p. 46, *"armament ever fitted to any warplane" / Ibid.*

p. 47, *"threatened to tear the plane apart"* / Baugher, Joe. "Convair B-36B Peacemaker."

p. 47, *"were in the U.S. nuclear arsenal"* / Correll, John T. *The Air Force and the Cold War*: p. 8.

p. 47, *"delivery platform for the atomic bomb" / Ibid.*

p. 48, *"massive 10,000-pound Fat Man nuclear device"* / Baugher, Joe. "Convair B-36B Peacemaker."

p. 48, *"drop of the payload" / Ibid.*

p. 48, "K-1 *compensated for crosswinds automatically" / "Ibid.*

p. 48, *"made it practically invincible at high altitude" / Ibid.*

p. 48, *"with a crew of thirty or forty sheet metal men"* / Ford, Daniel. "B-36: Bomber at the Crossroads."

p. 49, *"because the engines had sucked the sumps dry of all 150 gallons of oil" / Ibid.*

p. 49, *"mechanics always carried a bucket of spark plugs" / Ibid.*

p. 49, *"reversed in flight or on takeoff" / Ibid.*

p. 49, *"flexed for a few hundred hours, breaking the sealant" / Ibid.*

p. 50, *"Too large to fit in most hangers"* / Jenkins, Dennis R. *Convair B-36 Peacemaker*: p. 33.

p. 50, *"either subject to reconfiguration or awaiting modification" / Ibid.*, p. 38.

p. 51, "*We can thank the B-36 for preventing this*" / Pyeatt, Don. Untitled.

p. 51, *"that would make your hair stand on end"* / Ford, Daniel. "B-36: Bomber at the Crossroads."

p. 51, *"the infantry rather than fly on another B-36"* / *Ibid.*

p. 52, *"hence its code name"* / "Model of the Fat Man Bomb."

p. 52, *"a whole generation of early U.S. nuclear weapons"* / *Ibid.*

p. 53, *"deployment that was now being envisioned"* / "Weapons of mass destruction (WMD). Mark 4."

p. 53, *"high explosives trigger together"* / *Ibid.*

p. 53, *"deterrence arsenal at breakneck speed"* / *Ibid.*

p. 53, *"twice the power of the version dropped on Nagasaki"* / *Ibid.*

p. 54, *"Little Boy and Fat Man were not released to the public until the 1960s"* / "The First Atomic Bombs."

p. 54, *"of the interior of Fat Man are still sealed"* / *Ibid.*

CHAPTER THREE NOTES

p. 56, *"It wouldn't dare."* / Broyhill, Marvin T. "A Peaceful Profession."

p. 57, *"frequently to the point of rudeness"* / Boyne, Walter J. "LeMay."

p. 57, *"LeMay was going to be a flyer"* / "A Cold War & A Hot Bomb."

p. 57, *"Reserve Officers' Training Corps (ROTC), he became an officer"* / Boyne, Walter J. "LeMay."

p. 57, *"become a reserve officer in the Air Corps Reserve"* / *Ibid.*

p. 57, *"control stick, he held on"* / *Ibid.*

p. 58, *"logging more hours than any of his colleagues"* / *Ibid.*

p. 58, *"including celestial navigation and instrument flying"* / *Ibid.*

p. 58, *"were provided for the expenses of either flight or ground crews"* / *Ibid.*

p. 58, *"a promotion to First Lieutenant in March 1935"* / *Ibid.*

p. 59, *"delivering large payloads to distant targets"* / "History of the Strategic Air Command."

p. 59, *"General Head Quarters at Langley Field, Virginia"* / *Ibid.*

p. 59, *"different roles would make far more effective and lethal crew members"* / Boyne, Walter J. "LeMay."

p. 59, *"regime would help keep them alive"* / *Ibid.*

p. 60, "*Columbia in August of the same year*" / "History of the Strategic Air Command."

p. 60, "*successfully directed the mission*" / *Ibid.*

p. 60, "*all before the start of World War II*" / "Gen. Curtis E. LeMay."

p. 60, "*despaired that even their monopoly of the high seas was being challenged*" / Boyne, Walter J. "LeMay."

p. 60, "*squadron commander in the 34th Bombardment Group*" / *Ibid.*

p. 61, "*in every position on the B-17 except that of ball gunner*" / *Ibid.*

p. 61, "*avoid enemy fighters and anti-aircraft fire*" / *Ibid.*

p. 61, "*bombs on target than other bomber groups*" / *Ibid.*

p. 61, "*all their guns could deliver defensive fire on enemy fighters*" / *Ibid.*

p. 61, "*then by the B-29 Superfortresses in the Pacific*" / "Gen. Curtis E. LeMay."

p. 61, "*LeMay insisted on personally leading the toughest raids*" / Boyne, Walter J. "LeMay."

p. 61, "*located 500 miles behind enemy lines*" / Price, Alfred. "Against Resensburg and Schweinfurt."

p. 61, "*Of the 291 B-17s involved, only 93 returned intact*" / *Ibid.*

p. 61, "*in this racket it's the tough guys who lead the survivors*" / Boyne, Walter J. "LeMay."

p. 62, "*Guam headquarters in the Mariana Islands*" / *Ibid.*

p. 62, "*Chief of Staff of the Strategic Air Forces in the Pacific*" / *Ibid.*

p. 62, "*precision bombing of Japan to low-altitude, incendiary attacks*" / *Ibid.*

p. 62, "*on cottage industry with families making parts for the military in their homes*" / *Ibid.*

p. 63, "*delayed-fuse high explosive bombs to hamper firefighting efforts*" / "History of the Strategic Air Command."

p. 63, "*The bombing resulted in the world's first-known firestorm*" / *Ibid.*

p. 63, "*100,000 civilians and incinerated sixteen square miles of the city*" / *Ibid.*

p. 63, *"he fully expected to be tried for war crimes"* / McNamara, Robert S. "We Need Rules for War."

p. 63, *"single day the attack will have served its purpose"* / Henderson, David R. "Remembering Hiroshima."

p. 65, *"16 August 1945, the Japanese surrendered unconditionally"* / "History of the Strategic Air Command."

p. 66, *"Japanese Emperor the means to save face while surrendering"* / *Ibid.*

p. 66, *"Superfortress B-29 on a nonstop record flight from Japan to Chicago"* / "A Cold War & A Hot Bomb."

p. 66, *"melted down and recycled into aluminum ingots"* / "History of the Strategic Air Command."

p. 66, *"cherished B-29s were bulldozed over cliffs"* / *Ibid.*

p. 66, *"for leading the development of new technologies"* / Boyne, Walter J. "LeMay."

p. 67, *"America's first tactical offensive missiles"* / Cronley, T.J. "Curtis E. LeMay: The Enduring 'Big Bomber' Man."

p. 67, *"lived amid the rubble and despair of postwar Germany"* / *Ibid.*

p. 67, *"see the Iron Curtain descend across Europe"* / *Ibid.*

p. 68, *"freight and passenger trains and water traffic to Berlin"* / *Ibid.*

p. 68, *"cut off electricity to the city, claiming 'technical difficulties'"* / Boyne, Walter J. "General Curtis E. LeMay and Berlin Airlift."

p. 68, *"dedicate all his C-47s to an airlift to relieve Berlin"* / Cronley, T.J. "Curtis E. LeMay: The Enduring 'Big Bomber' Man."

p. 68, *"commandeered C-54s, C-47s and C-82s wherever he could find them"* / Boyne, Walter J. "General Curtis E. LeMay and the Berlin Airlift."

p. 68, *"flew gifts to the 10,000 children of Berlin"* / *Ibid.*

p. 68, *"Commanding General Army Air Forces may direct"* / "Weapons of mass destruction (WMD): Strategic Air Command."

p. 69, *"strategic, long-range air-combat operations"* / *Ibid.*

p. 69, *"headquartered at Bolling Field near Washington, D.C"* / "History of The Strategic Air Command. The start-up."

p. 69, *"days of the 500-plane raids common during World War II"* / *Ibid.*

p. 69, "SAC *deployed B-29s to only two groups"* / "History of The Strategic Air Command. The U.S. Air Force is Established."

p. 70, *"days of army airmen were gone forever"* / *Ibid.*

p. 70, *"more importantly, its mission"* / "Weapons of mass destruction (WMD): Strategic Air Command."

p. 70, *"of the reach of Soviet bombers"* / Cronley, T.J. "Curtis E. LeMay: The Enduring 'Big Bomber' Man."

p. 70, *"LeMay assumed command of SAC"* / Boyne, Walter J. "LeMay."

p. 70, *"in time of war than any other man in the world"* / *Ibid.*

p. 70, *"operational, and the crews were poorly trained"* / Cronley, T.J. "Curtis E. LeMay: The Enduring 'Big Bomber' Man."

p. 70, *"challenge LeMay had ahead of him"* / Ford, Daniel. "B-36: Bomber at the Crossroads.

p. 70, *"wrote of the SAC he inherited"* / *Ibid.*

p. 70, *"would dare not attack Western Europe"* / "Curtis LeMay: Demented Cold Warrior."

p. 70, *"no better than that available for the Soviet Union"* / Cronley, T.J. "Curtis E. LeMay: The Enduring 'Big Bomber' Man."

p. 70, *"ability to think analytically but still act operationally"* / "Flying with the A-Bomb on Board."

p. 71, *"theaters and restaurants to let headquarters know their location"* / "Weapons of Mass Destruction (WMD)" www.globalsecurity.org/wmd/library/report/1986/CTJ.htm. Accessed 8 August 2006.

p. 71, *"always on a war footing"* / *Ibid.*

p. 71, *"the milk deliveries would continue"* / Boyne, Walter J. "LeMay."

p. 71, *"often dragging their entire crews down with them"* / Cronley, T.J. "Curtis E. LeMay: The Enduring 'Big Bomber' Man."

p. 71, *"he made were soon adopted across the entire air force"* / Cronley, T.J. "Curtis E. LeMay: The Enduring 'Big Bomber' Man."

p. 71, *"single massive attack'—on Soviet cities within thirty days"* / Boyne, Walter J. "LeMay."

p. 72, *"the youngest since Ulysses S. Grant"* / "Gen. Curtis E. LeMay."

p. 72, *"America's intercontinental ballistic missile capability"* / Boyne, Walter J. "LeMay."

p. 72, *"the mightiest air force the world had ever known"* / *Ibid.*

p. 72, *"American airmen had never been higher"* / "Flying with the A-Bomb on Board."

p. 73, *"common, though none would admit it" / Ibid.*

p. 74, *"knowing that SAC was overhead" / Ibid.*

p. 74, *"It was a tough life" / Ibid.*

CHAPTER FOUR NOTES

p. 75, *"New York alone involved 101 B-29s"* / "7th Bombardment Wing Operations Carswell AFB, 1946–1948."

p. 75, *"over 600 times in a month"* / Pugliese, David. "The Downing of U.S. bomber 2075."

p. 75, *"Naval Range at Corpus Christi, Texas"* / "7th Bombardment Wing Operations Carswell AFB, 1946–1948."

p. 76, *"35,000 feet and one from 40,000 feet"* / Coker, William. "The Extra-Super Blockbuster."

p. 77, *"longest recorded to date in a B-36"* / "7th Bombardment Wing Operations Carswell AFB, 1949–1951."

p. 77, *"west runway lengthened to 14,500 feet"* / "Eielson AFB."

p. 77, *"pioneer Carl Ben Eielson" / Ibid.*

p. 77, *"42 minutes with 6 hours and 33 minutes"* / "Fairbanks, Alaska."

p. 77, *"examine the facilities at Eielson"* / "7th Bombardment Wing Operations Carswell AFB, 1949–1951."

p. 78, *"cold-weather capability of the B-36" / Ibid.*

p. 78, *"exercise was completed without problems"* / "The Military's Role in Nuclear Matters 1949–1952." Defense Nuclear Agency: p. 70.

p. 78, *"home bases in the continental United States"* / Ford, Daniel. "B-36: Bomber at the Crossroads."

p. 78, *"flying around the flag pole"* / Morris, Ted A. "Flying the Aluminum and Magnesium Overcast."

p. 78, "Europe or the Middle East" / "Convair B-36."

p. 79, *"Soviet Union for the following February"* / Pyeatt, Don. "Broken Arrow."

p. 79, "*and land at some other base or return [to Carswell]*" / Army Air Forces Report of Major Accident.

p. 79, "*bomb from the Atomic Energy Commission*" / Pugliese, David. "The Downing of U.S. bomber 2075."

p. 79, "*one of its four nuclear weapons storage sites*" / "Weapon Storage Sites: Q Areas."

p. 80, "*as real as it gets short of war*" / Pyeatt, Don. Untitled.

p. 80, "*defense forces stationed along the way*" / Roddick, Jim. "Gentle Giant."

p. 80, " *flight engineers, radio operator and gunners*" / Army Air Forces Report of Major Accident. Testimony of Lt. Col. Chadwell: p. 25.

p. 80, "*members of the crew*" / Army Air Forces Report of Major Accident. Testimony of Col. Blanchard: p. 36.

p. 82, "'*in all, a very fine trip up*'" / Army Air Forces Report of Major Accident. Testimony of Col. Bartlett: p. 251.

p. 83, "*permission for Bartlett to land*" / *Ibid.*: p. 252.

p. 83, "*two bomb bay fuel tank*" / *Ibid.*: p. 253.

p. 83, " *headed to their debriefing*" / Erickson, B.A. "It's Easy to Fly the B-36."

p. 83, "*bunk at the end of a very long day*" / Morris, Ted A. "Flying the Aluminum and Magnesium Overcast."

p. 83, "*nondescript briefing room at Eielson*" / Army Air Forces Report of Major Accident. Testimony of Col. Chadwell: p. 29.

p. 83, "*including night and high-altitude flying*" / Army Air Forces Report of Major Accident. Testimony of Col. Blanchard: p. 35.

p. 83, "14,000 *feet before climbing to* 40,000 *feet and continuing to Fort Peck, Montana*" / *Ibid.*: p. 27.

p. 84, "*head east to return home to Carswell AFB in Texas*" / Roddick, Jim. "Gentle Giant."

p. 84, "*extended only 12 miles off shore*" / "B-36 2075."

p. 84, "*icing conditions which were forecast*" / Army Air Forces Report of Major Accident. Testimony of Lt. Col. Roberts: p. 20.

p. 84, "*when it landed at Fort Worth, Texas*" / *Ibid.*

p. 84, *"touch down safely back at Carswell AFB"* / Army Air Forces Report of Major Accident. Testimony of Lt. Col. Chadwell: p. 32.

p. 84, *"15,000 feet and 'not much' icing at 17,000–18,000 feet"* / *Ibid.*: p. 26.

p. 84, *"crew members received approval to fly"* / *Ibid.*: p. 29.

p. 85, *"necessary for the implosion-type device"* / "Smithsonian and the Enola Gay: Atomic Bomb."

p. 85, *"dummy made of lead"* / Pyeatt, Don. Untitled.

p. 85, *"core were not installed for this flight"* / *Ibid.*

p. 85, *"preflight check involving six hundred separate steps"* / Ford, Daniel. "B-36: Bomber at the Crossroads."

p. 86, *"the airplane was in good condition"* / *"all of these [problems] were minor"* / Army Air Forces Report of Major Accident. Testimony of Col. Roberts: p. 16.

p. 86, *"lockers, drinking water and in-flight meals"* / Morris, Ted A. "Flying the Aluminum and Magnesium Overcast."

p. 86, *"Gibson Girl, was thrown aboard"* / Army Air Forces Report of Major Accident. Testimony of Lt. Col. Chadwell: p. 29.

p. 86, *"crew's location or follow the signal to its origin"* / Meulstee, Louis. "Gibson Girl."

p. 86, *"collected the final mission and weather information"* / Morris, Ted A. "Flying the Aluminum and Magnesium Overcast."

p. 86, *"engine power settings for all legs of the flight"* / *Ibid.*

p. 86, *"same procedure on the right wing"* / *Ibid.*

p. 87, *"Tempers frayed as takeoff time approached"* / *Ibid.*

p. 88, *"temperature of the hangar was approximately 32°F"* / Army Air Forces Report of Major Accident. Testimony of Capt. Baulch: p. 48.

p. 89, *"He gave the all-clear and clambered aboard"* / Erickson, B.A. "It's easy to fly the B-36."

p. 89, *"standard operating procedure"* / Morris, Ted A. "Flying the Aluminum and Magnesium Overcast."

p. 90, *"and unlocked the flight controls"* / Erickson, B.A. "It's easy to fly the B-36."

p. 90, *"cargo lumbered down the runway"* / Morris, Ted A. "Flying the Aluminum and Magnesium Overcast."

p. 91, *"cargo off the runway at 140 miles per hour"* / Army Air Forces Report of Major Accident. Description of the Accident: p. 4C.

p. 91, *"de-icing heat while the plane was on the ground" / Ibid.*

p. 91, *"with a thin skin of ice on the outside panels"* / Army Air Forces Report of Major Accident. Testimony of Capt. Barry: p. 63.

p. 91, *"with the propellers turning for takeoff"* / Morris, Ted A. "Flying the Aluminum and Magnesium Overcast."

p. 91, *"without the water injection system"* / Army Air Forces Report of Major Accident. Testimony of Capt. Baulch: p. 44.

p. 92, *"Cox then maintained takeoff power for four minutes"* / Army Air Forces Report of Major Accident. Testimony of 1st Lt. Ernest O. Cox: p. 103.

p. 92, *"set the gas valves in the flight position"* / Army Air Forces Report of Major Accident. Testimony of Capt. Barry: p. 56.

p. 92, *"relayed my reports for me and we worked out OK on that" / Ibid.*: p. 56.

p. 92, *"Darrah into the wings to manually open it" / Ibid.*

p. 92, *"whether we had turned that off at any time or not" / Ibid.*

p. 93, *"plane manually in an effort to correct the problem"* / Army Air Forces Report of Major Accident. Testimony of 1st Lt. Ernest O. Cox.

p. 93, *"was for only a few seconds this continued" / Ibid.*

p. 93, *"Aldis Lamps 'were not to be found.'"* / Army Air Forces Report of Major Accident. Testimony of 1st Lt. Ernest O. Cox: p. 75.

p. 93, *"Any attempt to lean them above idle cut-off would fail"* / Ricketts, Bruce. "Broken Arrow."

p. 94, *"Why not? It didn't work anyway"* / Roddick, Jim. "Gentle Giant."

p. 94, *"climb above the icing conditions"* / Army Air Forces Report of Major Accident. Testimony of Capt. Barry.

CHAPTER FIVE NOTES

p. 95, "*see the engines from their seats in the cockpit*" / Roddick, Jim. "Gentle Giant."

p. 95, "*Commander Barry ordered the engine shut down*" / *Ibid.*

p. 95, "*power of the three engines on the right wing*" / "Reflections."

p. 95, "*It windmilled backward*" / Army Air Forces Report of Major Accident. Testimony of 1st Lt. Ernest O. Cox.

p. 96, "*altitude at a rate of 500 feet per minute (fpm)*" / Army Air Forces Report of Major Accident. Testimony of Capt. Barry.

p. 96, "*broadcast of an emergency distress signal*" / Ibid.

p. 96, "*Queen Charlotte Island Sound and Vancouver Island*" / Pugliese, David. "The Downing of U.S. bomber 2075."

p. 96, "*apply emergency power to the remaining three engines*" / Roddick, Jim. "Gentle Giant."

p. 97, "*impossibility, trying to keep the giant bomber aloft*" / Army Air Forces Report of Major Accident. Testimony of Capt. Barry.

p. 97, "*uncertain whether the radio was operating*" / Pyeatt, Don. Untitled.

p. 97, "*we knew that we had to make plans for leaving the aircraft*" / *Ibid.*

p. 97, "*engines caught fire, it was time to leave*" / "Nightmare at midnight." http://www.cowtown.net/proweb/nightmare.htm. Accessed.

p. 97, "*going to ditch in Queen Charlotte Sound*" / Pugliese, David. "The Downing of U.S. bomber 2075."

p. 98, "*dirty bomb and spread radiation in a large radius*" / Roddick, Jim. "Gentle Giant."

p. 98, "*technology packed into the Fat Man's casing remained top secret*" / Pugliese, David. "The Downing of U.S. bomber 2075."

p. 98, "*their position relative to the civilian population on the ground*" / Pyeatt, Don. Untitled.

p. 98, "*the waters of the strait appeared below*" / Pugliese, David. "The Downing of U.S. bomber 2075."

p. 99, "*reduced to fragments at the bottom of the ocean*" / *Ibid.*

p. 99, *"detonators were secure in their predetermined places on the bomb"* / Borutski, Barry. "Cold War relic B-36B."

p. 99, *"Nothing happened. He hit the switch again"* / Army Air Forces Report of Major Accident. Testimony of Capt. Barry.

p. 100, *"seeing the flash as it exploded"* / Pyeatt, Don. Untitled.

p. 100, *"remembered seeing the clouds light up"* / Roddick, Jim. "Gentle Giant."

p. 100, *"and knocked him off balance"* / Borutski, Barry. "Cold War relic B-36B."

p. 100, *"six-person life rafts from the B-36 fleet"* / Army Air Forces Report of Major Accident. Testimony of Capt. Barry.

p. 100, *"we got over land we were at 5,000 feet"* / Army Air Forces Report of Major Accident. Testimony of Capt. Barry.

p. 101, *"slightly east of south and into the strong 55-knot headwind"* / Roddick, Jim. "Gentle Giant."

p. 102, *"sides of the plane to provide openings from which to exit"* / Pyeatt, Don. Untitled.

p. 102, *"was so tight in front that I fastened it under the Mae West"* / Roddick, Jim. "Gentle Giant."

p. 102, *"so high you break your back leaning over"* / Army Air Forces Report of Major Accident. Testimony of S/Sgt. Thrasher.

p.102, *"a steady signal to locate the downed bomber"* / Roddick, Jim. "Gentle Giant."

p. 102, *"and that is one reason I wanted [the crew] out"* / Army Air Forces Report of Major Accident. Testimony of Capt. Barry.

p. 102, *"I ordered the crew to bail out, and away they went"* / Roddick, Jim. "Gentle Giant."

p. 102, *"Trippodi, Pooler, MacDonald and Gerhart"* / Perkins, Frank. "Nightmare at midnight."

p. 103, *"Thrasher received the order to abandon ship"* / Roddick, Jim. "Gentle Giant."

p. 103, *"Princess Royal Island, and to go ahead and bail out"* / *Ibid.*

p. 103, *"on the bottom of the left side"* / *Ibid.*

p. 103, *"ignored the rules; he simply dove out head first"* / *Ibid.*

p. 103, *"bang your head against the plane or injure yourself"* / Army Air Forces Report of Major Accident. Testimony of S/Sgt Thrasher Left Scanner 26 February 1953.

p. 103, *"Stephens kicked me free. He saved my life"* / Roddick, Jim. "Gentle Giant."

p. 103, *"still had a few minutes to think things over before [he] hit"* / Army Air Forces Report of Major Accident. Testimony of S/Sgt Thrasher.

p. 104, *"emergency equipment in the shadows of the cramped forward cabin"* / Roddick, Jim. "Gentle Giant."

p. 104, *"Schreier 'hurriedly removing his vest'"* / Pyeatt, Don. Untitled.

p. 104, *"The time was five minutes past midnight"* / Roddick, Jim. "Gentle Giant."

p. 104, *"'No one knows if he did or did not jump,' he would later remark"* / Pyeatt, Don. Untitled.

p. 105, *"I cleared the propeller by a good many feet"* / Army Air Forces Report of Major Accident. Testimony of Capt. Barry.

p. 105, *"he was jerked upward in the strong wind"* / Ibid.

p. 107, *"But I don't know where she crashed"* / Roddick, Jim. "Gentle Giant."

CHAPTER SIX NOTES

p. 113, *"the paper ran a photo of a B-36"* / Roddick, Jim. "Gentle Giant."

p. 113, *"was carrying two extra crew members" / Ibid.*

p. 114, *"Superfortresses are covering the area from the air" / Ibid.*

p. 114, *"Mark IV nuclear weapon or its core, plutonium or otherwise"* / Pugliese, David. "The Downing of U.S. bomber 2075."

p. 114, *"on the ground. I cut myself free with a knife"* / Roddick, Jim. "Gentle Giant."

p. 114, *"he witnessed the bomber circle back over him"* / Army Air Forces Report of Major Accident. Testimony of S/Sgt. Thrasher.

p. 114, *"he pulled his parachute from the tree"* / Terry Kay, "Hell Comes to a B-36."

p. 114, *"all of his heavy arctic clothing and a pair of Eskimo mukluks"* / *Ibid.*

p. 115, *"himself in his parachute and tried to sleep"* / *Ibid.*

p. 115, *""I landed in a little pond with a thin ice crust on it," he reported"* / Roddick, Jim. "Gentle Giant."

p. 115, *"about 3 feet had melted through"* / Army Air Forces Report of Major Accident. Testimony of Capt. Barry.

p. 115, *"landed within shouting distance of me"* / *Ibid.*

p. 115, *"I fell onto a steep slope and started rolling downhill"* / Pyeatt, Don. Untitled.

p. 115, *"but I had missed them all"* / Roddick, Jim. "Gentle Giant."

p. 116, *"we remained cold and wet until we were rescued"* / Pyeatt, Don. Untitled.

p. 116, *"It was nothing short of a miracle"* / Roddick, Jim. "Gentle Giant."

p. 116, *"crawled under it and went to sleep"* / *Ibid.*

p. 116, *"kept him dry through the night"* / *Ibid.*

p. 116, *"I tried to build a fire but couldn't"* / *Ibid.*

p. 116, *"where he settled in to wait for rescue"* / Perkins, Frank. "Nightmare at midnight."

p. 116, *"and never would have got hung up"* / Roddick, Jim. "Gentle Giant."

p. 116, *"whistle being blown repeatedly"* / *Ibid.*

p. 117, *"reunion and then moved downhill"* / Pyeatt, Don. Untitled.

p. 117, *"But the rescue crew never saw his signal and flew away"* / Perkins, Frank. "Nightmare at midnight."

p. 117, *"they once again started for the coast"* / Roddick, Jim. "Gentle Giant."

p. 117, *"I wanted to wrap myself in it"* / *Ibid.*

p. 117, *"was happy to find Gerhart there as well"* / Terry Kay, "Hell Comes to a B-36.": p. 41.

p. 118, *"they got the fire going"* / Roddick, Jim. "Gentle Giant."

p. 118, *"search we spotted Trippodi hanging upside down"* / Pyeatt, Don. Untitled.

p. 118, *"he would not be able to walk to the coast" / Ibid.*

p. 118, *"own jacket to warm them and restart the circulation"* / Terry Kay, "Hell Comes to a B-36": p. 41.

p. 118, *"fever and was almost delirious from shock"* / Pyeatt, Don. Untitled.

p. 118, *"person will often not survive the journey" / Ibid.*

p. 119, *"but they would come back for me"* / Perkins, Frank. "Nightmare at midnight."

p. 119, *"When morning came, we decided to try to walk"* / Roddick, Jim. "Gentle Giant."

p. 119, *"The tracks led them closer and closer to the coast" / Ibid.*

p. 119, *"more visible from the air"* / Pyeatt, Don. Untitled.

p. 119, *"gathering wood to build the fire higher"* / Roddick, Jim. "Gentle Giant."

p. 119, *"like a plane, then we decided it was a boat" / Ibid.*

p. 119, *"disappearing behind a point of land"* / Terry Kay, "Hell Comes to a B-36": p. 42.

p. 119, *"dying on this remote island in central British Columbia" / Ibid.*

p. 120, *"course to run closer to the shore"* / Roddick, Jim. "Gentle Giant."

p. 120, *"The rescuers found Cox, Darrah and Schuler"* / Terry Kay, "Hell Comes to a B-36": p. 42.

p. 120, *"and his group huddled around their fire"* / Roddick, Jim. "Gentle Giant."

p. 120, *"bail out of any ship, let alone in a gale, at midnight" / Ibid.*

p. 120, *"for I fully expected to spend another night in the snow" / Ibid.*

p. 120, *"They began the difficult job of carrying him back to the* Cayuga." / *Ibid.*

p. 121, *"Then I drank all their cocoa" / Ibid.*

p. 122, *"the crew of the* Cayuga *found Pooler"* / Perkins, Frank. "Nightmare at midnight."

p. 122, *"chocolate a day, I could eat for nine days" / Ibid.*

p. 122, *"while, he wouldn't talk about it anymore"* / Roddick, Jim. "Gentle Giant."

p. 122, *"rescued crew were in newspapers around the world" / Ibid.*

p. 122, "*Again, handle this with care. No leaks*" / *Ibid.*

p. 123, "*To hell with it*" / Perkins, Frank. "Nightmare at midnight."

CHAPTER SEVEN NOTES

p. 125, "*on a routine training flight*" / Pugliese, David. "The Downing of U.S. bomber 2075."

p. 125, "*nuclear weapons at any specific location*" / Department of the Navy. OPNAV Instruction 5721.1F.

p. 125, "*specific ships, submarines or aircraft*" / *Ibid.*

p. 125, "*After all, it was their nuclear bomb that was missing*" / Pugliese, David. "The Downing of U.S. bomber 2075."

p. 125, "'*what the hell they did with one of our atomic weapons,' he stated bluntly*" / *Ibid.*

p. 127, "*did not contain the plutonium core when it was destroyed*" / *Ibid.*

p. 127, "*engine problems that had led to the crash*" / *Ibid.*

p. 127, "*weather conditions that may be encountered in flight*" / Army Air Forces Report of Major Accident.

p. 128, "*exhaust systems that eventually ignited, causing the fires*" / Pyeatt, Don. Untitled.

p. 128, "*never talked to reporters about anything*" / *Ibid.*

p. 128, "*aircraft missing since yr. 1950 enroute [from] Eielson [to] McChord*" / Army Air Forces Report of Major Accident.

p. 128, " *British Columbia, some 50 miles from the Alaska border*" / Roddick, Jim. "Gentle Giant."

p. 128, "*but Ellis Hall and his airplane were never seen again*" / *Ibid.*

p. 129, "*had rigged the detonators to the Mark IV nuclear bomb on Ship 2075*" / Borutski, Barry. "Cold War relic B-36B."

p. 129, "*search for the remains of missing crewmembers*" / *Ibid.*

p. 129, "*team that would work its way up Mount Kologet*" / *Ibid.*

p. 129, "*could not reach it, neither could the Soviets*" / *Ibid.*

p. 130, "*Skyway Air, a small charter airline, fit the bill perfectly*" / Roddick, Jim. "Gentle Giant."

p. 130, *"USAF received the full and immediate cooperation of the Canadian government" / Ibid.*

p. 130, *"The flaps were up"* / Clearwater, John. "Diary."

p. 131, *"gear was retracted and the nose gear was facing the nose" / Ibid.*

p. 131, *"bomber had not been attempting to land at the time of the crash" / Ibid.*

p. 131, *"bombsights and other sensitive electronic equipment"* / Roddick, Jim. "Gentle Giant."

p. 131, *"three engines across a small ridge 500 yards away"* / Davidge, Doug. "Environmental Impact Study."

p. 131, *"destroyed the main landing gear, forward bomb bays and cockpit" / Ibid.*

p. 131, *"nothing identifiable of the forward structure" / Ibid.*

p. 131, *"rations, mess kits, bayonets and flashlights"* / Borutski, Barry. "Cold War relic B-36B."

p. 131, *"Goodrich survival suits and life rafts" / Ibid.*

p. 132, *"had loaded a body bag into the waiting transport"* / Roddick, Jim. "Gentle Giant."

p. 132, *"grenades and another canister of dynamite sticks" / Ibid.*

p. 133, *"attached to it, H.L. Barry Captain AO-808341" / Ibid.*

p. 133, *"existed in the middle of British Columbia's pristine wilderness" / Ibid.*

p. 134, *"recovery team had removed a body back in 1954" / Ibid.*

p. 134, *"crewman had been found in the wreckage"* / Pugliese, David. "The Downing of U.S. bomber 2075."

p. 134, *"have traveled with the bomb, in case the weapon was needed in short order" / Ibid.*

p. 134, *"radioactive contamination and other dangerous goods"* / Davidge, Doug. "Environmental Impact Study."

p. 135, *"along with an aircrew, visited the B-36 crash site"* / Roddick, Jim. "Gentle Giant."

p. 135, *"All survey team members were issued accumulative radiation detectors"* / Davidge, Doug. "Environmental Impact Study."

p. 135, *"The aircraft electronics and gauges were the only radiation sources detected"* / *Ibid.*

p. 136, *"small arms rounds and the barrels of high explosives left by the USAF crash-site investigation and demolition team"* / *Ibid.*

p. 136, *"in the hope of finding their original owners"* / *Ibid.*

p. 136, *"the crash site a historic site under provincial heritage legislation"* / *Ibid.*

p. 136, *"who had been a gunner on Ship 2075 that night back in February 1950."* / Roddick, Jim. "Gentle Giant."

p. 137, *"Straley and Pollard, who jumped just before him"* / *Ibid.*

p. 137, *"that stormy night forty-six years earlier"* / *Ibid.*

p. 137, *"odd-looking freight, but he was in a hurry and wasn't curious"* / *Ibid.*

p. 137, *"the box and Deaver were on their way to Connecticut"* / *Ibid.*

p. 138, *"watchful eyes of the Atomic Energy Commission"* / Interview with Scott Deaver by Norman Leach, August 2006.

p. 138, *"like the Grand Slam bomb"* / Clearwater, John. "Diary."

p. 138, *"racks outfitted for conventional bombing with standard high explosive ordinance and survival kits"* / *Ibid.*

p. 138, *"gear strewn downhill of the bomb bays"* / *Ibid.*

CHAPTER EIGHT NOTES

p. 142, *"the courts have long recognized that eyewitness identification evidence is 'inherently unreliable'"* / Rohrer, Finlo. "The Problem with Eyewitnesses."

p. 143, *"saw and another source of information"* / *Ibid.*

p. 143, *"of the B-36 on that wintry afternoon at Eielson AFB"* / Roddick, Jim. "Gentle Giant."

p. 143, *"was the first to involve a missing nuclear bomb"* / Clearwater, John. "Diary."

p. 144, *"was equipped with regular bomb racks"* / *Ibid.*

p. 145, *"the weaponeer was to transfer the core to the bomb"* / "Howard E Goodwin."

p. 145, *"from the birdcage to the bomb was not aboard the bomber"* / Pyeatt, Don. Untitled.

p. 145, *"indicate that there was nothing not explainable on that site"* / Pugliese, David. "The Downing of U.S. bomber 2075."

p. 146, *"the sound would have been deafening"* / *Ibid.*

p. 146, *"the report on the original crash are still classified top-secret"* / *Ibid.*

p. 146, *"operation itself would have survived, and this would reveal U.S. nuclear war plans"* / Clearwater, John. "B-36 Bomber Crash in British Columbia."

p. 146, *"to bury or list the dead in the same grave"* / Moe, Doug. "Surprise deepens pilot mystery."

Bibliography

"7th Bombardment Wing Operations Carswell AFB, 1949–1951." 7th Bomb Wing B-36 Association. http://www.7bwb-36assn.org/b36genhistpg1.html. Accessed 25 February 2007.

"7th Bombardment Wing Operations, Carswell AFB, 1946–1948." 7th Bomb Wing B-36 Association. http://www.7bwb-36assn.org/b36genhistpg1.html. Accessed 29 March 2006.

Adams, Chris. *Inside the Cold War: A Cold Warrior's Reflections.* Maxwell AFB: Air UP, 1999.

Ah Xiang. "Chinese Civil Wars." http://www.republicanchina.org/civil_wars.html. Accessed 8 August 2006.

Air Force Association Special Report. The Air Force and the Cold War. Arlington VA: Aerospace Education Foundation, 2005.

"Armed Services Battle it Out over the B-36 Airplane." *Life* 6 June 1949.

Ascani, Lt. Col. Fred J. "Big an' Mighty B-36." *Skyways Magazine* January 1949.

"B-36 2075." http://b.36.2075.en.infoax.com. Accessed 10 August 2006.

"B-36 Pacemaker: Big, Bad and Beautiful." BBC-h2g2. 19 July 2005. http://www.bbc.co.uk/dna/h2g2/A4175219. Accessed 25 September 2006.

Barlow, Jeffery G. *Revolt of the Admirals: The Fight for Naval Aviation.* Washington: Naval Historical Center, 1995.

"Baruch Plan." http://www.bookrags.com/Baruch_Plan. Accessed 8 August 2006.

Baugher, Joe. "Convair B-36B Peacemaker." http://home.att.net/~jbaugher2/b36_5.html. Accessed 29 March 2006.

Borutski, Barry. "Cold War relic B-36B." *Flight Journal* December 2000. http://www.findarticles.com/p/articles/mi_qa3897/is_200012/ai_n8911612/pg_2. Accessed 31 March 2006.

Boyne, Walter J. "General Curtis E. LeMay and Berlin Airlift." www.konnections.com/airlift/clemay.htm. Accessed 4 August 2006.

—— "LeMay." *Air Force Magazine* March 1998. http://www.afa.org/magazine/March1998/0398LeMay.asp. Accessed 29 March 2006.

Broyhill, Marvin T. A *Peaceful Profession.* Petersburg VA: Strategic Air Command, 2001. http://www.strategic-air-command.com/gallery/downloads/sac305.doc. Accessed 26 September 2006.

Butler, Don. "For King, The Gouzenko affair was like a bomb." *Ottawa Citizen* 26 Oct 2005. http://www.canada.com/ottawa/ottawacitizen/news/story.html?id=d875f76c-da5b-4cc8-a244-9e9f30e04225. Accessed 29 March 2006.

"Civilian Control of Atomic Energy (1945–1946)." *The Manhattan Project: An Interactive History*. U.S. Dept. of Energy. http://www.cfo.doe.gov/me70/manhattan/civilian_control.htm. Accessed 30 March 2006.

Clearwater, John. *Canadian Nuclear Weapons: The Untold Story of Canada's Cold War Arsenal*. Toronto: The Dundurn Group, 1998.

—— *U.S. Nuclear Weapons in Canada*. Toronto: The Dundurn Group, 1999.

—— "B-36 Bomber Crash in British Columbia." Response to Canadian Press wire service article posted at "Peace BC: 1950 Bomber Crash in BC." 12 November 1998. Alberni Environmental Action Coalition.
http://www.portaec.net/library/peace/1950_bomber_crash_in_bc.html.
Accessed 15 August 2006.

—— "Diary of the expedition to recover nuclear weapons artifacts from the world's first Broken Arrow 27 August – 3 September 2003."
http://web.ncf.ca/da710/LostNukeExped.html
Accessed 1 August 2006.

Coker, William S. "The Extra-Super Blockbuster." *Air University Review* March–April 1967.

"Cold War 1945–1990."
http://www.u-s-history.com/pages/h1881.html.
Accessed 12 April 2006.

"A Cold War & A Hot Bomb."
http://www.nebraskastudies.org/0900/frameset_reset.html.
Accessed 29 March 2006.

"Convair B-36."
http://www.b-36peacemakermuseum.org/.
Accessed 25 September 2006.

Correll, John T. *The Air Force and the Cold War.* Arlington VA: Aerospace Education Foundation, 2005.

Cronley, T.J. Major. *Curtis E LeMay: The Enduring Big Bomber Man.* Quantico VA: Marine Corps Development and Education Command, 1986. Weapons of Mass Destruction (WMD). www.globalsecurity.org/wmd/library/report/1986/CTJ.htm. Accessed 8 August 2006.

"Curtis LeMay: Demented Cold Warrior."
http://www.geocities.com/lemaycurtis.
Accessed 11 August 2006.

"Czechoslovakia Coup of 1948."
http://www.globalsecurity.org/military/world/war/czechoslovakia.htm.
Accessed 8 August 2006.

"Damage Caused by Atomic Bombs."
http://mothra.rerf.or.jp/ENG/A-bomb/History/Damages.html.
Accessed 8 August 2006.

Davidge, Doug. "Environmental Impact Study of crash site of USAF bomber."
http://www.cowtown.net/proweb/brokenarrow2.htm.
Accessed 1 August 2006.

Davies, D.P. *Handling the Big Jets.* London: Civil Aviation Authority, 1973.

Defense Threat Reduction Agency, U.S. Department of Defense "Defences Nuclear Agency 1947–1997." Chapter Two "Military's Role in Nuclear Matters 1949–1952." Washington D.C. p. 70.
http://www.dtra.mil/newsservices/publications/pub_includes/docs/DefensesNuclearAgency.pdf
Accessed May 2006.

De Long, Bradford, and Barry Eichengreen. "The Marshall Plan: History's Most Successful Structural Adjustment Program." October 1991. http://www.econ.ucdavis.edu/faculty/alolmstead/DeLong.pdf. Accessed 8 August 2006.

De Long, Bradford J. *The Marshall Plan: History's Most Successful Structural Adjustment Program.* Cambridge MA: Harvard UP, 1991.

Deaver, Scott. Interview by Norman Leach.

Department of the Navy. Office of the Chief of Naval Operations. OPNAV Instruction 5721.1F. 3 February 2006.

Dodson, John T. "The B-36 Global Bomber." *Flying* July 1949.

"Eielson AFB." http://www.globalsecurity.org/military/facility/eielson.htm. Accessed 26 August 2006.

Erickson, B.A. "It's Easy to Fly the B-36." *Flying* April 1951.

"Fairbanks, Alaska." http://hometownusa.com/ak/Fairbanks.html\. Accessed 25 February 2007.

"First Atomic Bombs." http://www.islaiscreek.org/firstatomicbombsf.html.

"First Flight of XB-36 Judged Excellent." *Science Newsletter* 24 August 1946.

"Flying with the A-Bomb on Board." http://www.nebraskastudies.org/0900/stories/0901_0123.html. Accessed 11 August 2006.

Ford, Daniel. "B-36: Bomber at the Crossroads." *Air & Space Magazine* April 1996. http://www.airspacemag.com/ASM/Mag/Index/1996/AM/bacr.html. Accessed 29 March 2006.

Foreman, Jonathan. "The Day America Nuked Canada." *National Security* 17 March 2006.

Freedman, Lawrence. *The Cold War.* London: Cassell & Co., 2001.

"Gen. Curtis E. LeMay." http://www.nationalmuseum.af.mil/factsheets/factsheet.asp?id=1115. Accessed 29 March 2006.

Hansen, Chuck. "The Swords of Armageddon: U.S. Nuclear Weapons Development Since 1945." CD-ROM. Sunnyvale CA: Chukelea Publications, 1995.

"Harry Truman and the Truman Doctrine." Truman Presidential Museum and Library. http://www.trumanlibrary.org/teacher/doctrine.htm. Accessed 8 August 2006.

Hehs, Eric. "Beryl Arthur Erickson, Test Pilot." *Code One Magazine* October 1992.

Henderson, David R. "Remembering Hiroshima." http://www.antiwar.com/henderson/?articleid=9443. Accessed 26 September 2006.

"History of The Strategic Air Command. The start-up." http://www.strategic-air-command.com/history/history-02.htm. Accessed 29 March 2006.

"History of The Strategic Air Command. The U.S. Air Force is Established." http://www.strategic-air-command.com/history/history-03.htm. Accessed 29 March 2006.

"History of the Strategic Air Command." http://www.strategic-air-command.com/history/history-01.htm. Accessed 29 March 2006.

"Howard E Goodwin." New England Air Museum: 58th Bomb Wing Memorial.
http://www.neam.org/profile.asp?ID=615.
Accessed 13 August 2006.

Jacobsen, Meyers K., and Ray Wagner. *B-36 in Action.* Carrollton TX.: Squadron/Signal Publications, 1980.

Jacobsen, Meyers K. *Convair B-36: A Comprehensive History of America's Big Stick.* Atglen PA: Schiffer Military Books, 1998.

Jenkins, Dennis R. *Convair B-36 Peacemaker.* North Branch MN: Specialty P, 1999.

—— *Magnesium Overcast.* North Branch MN: Specialty P, 2001.

Johnsen, Frederick. *Thundering Peacemaker: The B-36 in Words and Pictures.* Tacoma WA: Bomber Books, 1978.

Jonas, George. "The Secret Garden: A defection by Russian code clerk Igor Gouzenko 50 years ago in Canada started the Cold War." *National Review* 9 Oct 1995.
http://www.findarticles.com/p/articles/mi_m1282/is_n19_v47/ai_17550673.
Accessed 29 March 2006.

Kay, Terry. "Hell Comes to a B-36." *Skyways Magazine* March 1951.

"Kennan's Long Telegram." *Cold War, Episode 2: Iron Curtain.* CNN Interactive.
http://www.cnn.com/SPECIALS/cold.war/episodes/02/documents/kennan.
Accessed 8 August 20.

Kennedy, Bruce. "Broken Arrows and Bent Spears." CNN Interactive, 2001.
http://www.cnn.com/SPECIALS/2000/democracy/nuclear/stories/accidents/.

"Klaus Fuchs (1911–1988)." *The American Experience: Race for the Super Bomb.* PBS. http://www.pbs.org/wgbh/amex/bomb/peopleevents/pandeAMEX54.html. Accessed 8 August 2006.

Kunsman, David M., and Douglas B. Lawson. *A Primer on U.S. Strategic Nuclear Policy.* Albuquerque: Sandia National Laboratories, 2001.

LeMay, Curtis. *Mission with LeMay.* Garden City NY: Doubleday, 1965.

Lewis, Andrew. *The Revolt of the Admirals.* Maxwell AFB: Air UP, 1998.

Manhattan Engineer District. "The Atomic Bombings of Hiroshima and Nagasaki." 29 June 1946. http://www.cddc.vt.edu/host/atomic/hiroshim/hiro_med.pdf. Accessed 8 August 2006.

McNamara, Robert S. "We Need Rules for War." *Los Angeles Times* 3 August 2003. http://www.wagingpeace.org/articles/2003/08/03_mcnamara_rules-for-war.htm. Accessed 26 September 2006.

Meulstee, Louis. "Gibson Girl: Evolution in Air-Sea Rescue Radio Transmitters." http://wftw.nl/gibsongirl/gibsongirl.html. Accessed 30 March 2006.

"Military's Role in Nuclear Matters 1949–1952." Defense Nuclear Agency: p. 70.

"Model of the Fat Man Bomb." http://www.atomicarchive.com/Movies/Movie3.shtml. Accessed 27 September 2006.

Moe, Doug. "Surprise deepens pilot mystery." *Capital Times* (Madison WI) 20 November 2004. http://www.madison.com/tct/opinion/column/moe/index.php?ntid=18726&ntpid=2. Accessed 12 August 2006.

Morris, Ted A. "Flying the Aluminum and Magnesium Overcast." http://www.zianet.com/tmorris/b36.html. Accessed 29 March 2006.

Myers, Peter. "Pavel Sudoplatov, Special Tasks." 6 September 2001. http://users.cyberone.com.au/myers/sudoplat.html. Accessed 23 September 2006.

NATO. "1948." 6 Nov 2001. http://www.nato.int/docu/update/45-49/1948e.htm. Accessed 8 August 2006.

—— "The North Atlantic Treaty." 4 April 1949. NATO Basic Texts. http://www.nato.int/docu/basictxt/treaty.htm. Accessed 8 August 2006.

Peluso, Tony. "The Formation of NATO." August 1998. http://novaonline.nvcc.edu/eli/evans/his135/Events/nato49/nato49.html. Accessed 8 August 2006.

Perkins, Frank. "Nightmare at midnight." *Fort Worth Star-Telegram* 16 Feb. 1997. Rpt http://www.cowtown.net/proweb/nightmare.htm. Accessed 31 March 2006.

Price, Alfred. "Against Resensburg and Schweinfurt." *Airforce Magazine* September 1993. http://www.afa.org/magazine/1993/0993Against.html. Accessed 28 September 2006.

Pugliese, David. "The Downing of U.S. bomber 2075." *Ottawa Citizen* 13 Feb 2000. Rpt. at Canadian Coalition for Nuclear Responsibility website. http://www.ccnr.org/news/news_briefs_56.html#4. Accessed 15 August 2006.

Pyeatt, Don. "Broken Arrow." http://www.cowtown.net/proweb/brokenarrow1.htm. Accessed 29 March 2006.

—— Untitled. [Co-Pilot's Interview] http://www.cowtown.net/proweb/brokenarrow3.htm. Accessed 29 March 2006.

Reece, Wayne. "B-36 Peacemaker Memories." Peacemaker Museum 11 June 2003. http://www.b-36peacemakermuseum.org/Articles/reece.htm.

"Reflections." 7th Bomb Wing B-36 Association. http://www.7bwb-36assn.org/reflect.html. Accessed 31 March 2006.

Ricketts, Bruce. "Broken Arrow, A Lost Nuclear Weapon in Canada." Mysteries of Canada. http://www.mysteriesofcanada.com/BC/broken_arrow.htm. Accessed 28 February 2007.

"Rise of the Nuclear Age." Open Society's Archive. http://www.osa.ceu.hu/guide/rip/10/TheExhibitionI.html. Accessed 8 August 2006.

Roddick, Jim. "The Gentle Giant: Our Resident Atomic Bomber." Geostories. The Geological Association of Canada – Corderillan Section. http://gac-cs.ca/media/pdfs/geostories/GentleGiant.pdf. Accessed 12 August 2006.

Rohrer, Finlo. "The Problem with Eyewitnesses." BBC News. 24 August 2005.
http://news.bbc.co.uk/2/hi/uk_news/4177082.stm.
Accessed 1 August 2006.

SAC *Manual 50–35: Aircraft Performance Engineers Manual for the B-36 Aircraft Engine Operation*. January 1952.

School of Advanced Airpower Studies. *The Paths of Heaven: The Evolution of Airpower Theory*. Maxwell AFB: Air UP, 1997.

"Smithsonian and the Enola Gay: Atomic Bomb." Air Force Association.
http://www.afa.org/new_root/enolagay/AB.asp.
Accessed 3 March 2007.

Steury, Donald P. "How the CIA Missed Stalin's Bomb." *Studies in Intelligence* unclassified edition 49.1 2005.
https://www.cia.gov/csi/studies/vol49no1/html_files/stalins_bomb_3.html.
Accessed 8 August 2006.

"Strategic Air Command has its Big Planes Ready for Intercontinental War." *Life* 27 August 1951.

Sudoplatov, Pavel, and Anatoli Sudoplatov. *Special Tasks: The Memoirs of an Unwanted Witness; A Soviet Spymaster*. London: Little Brown, 1994.

Terry Kay, "Hell Comes to a B-36," *Skyways* March 1951.

"Truman Doctrine Speech." *Cold War, Episode 3: Marshall Plan*. CNN Interactive.
http://www.cnn.com/SPECIALS/cold.war/episodes/03/documents/truman/.
Accessed 8 August 2006.

Tweedie, Neil and Peter Day. "Arrogance of the atom spy who expected to go back to his job" *London Telegraph* 22 May 2003. http://www.telegraph.co.uk/news/main.jhtml?xml=/news/2003/05/22/narch22.xml. Accessed 29 March 2006.

United States Air Force. *Flight Handbook, USAF Series, B-36H-III Aircraft.* 26 November 1954.

United States Army Air Force. *Emergency Uses of the Parachute, AAF Manual* No. 64-15. February 1945.

—— *Handbook of Instructions for Packing and Maintenance: Type B-8 Parachute,* T.O. No. 13-5-5. 10 September 1943.

—— *Operation and Service Instructions: Parachutes Conventional Type Man Carrying,* T.O. No. 13-5-2. 15 May 1943.

—— *Report of Major Accident.* Carswell Air Force Base, TX: February 1950.

"United States Considered Using Atomic Bomb in Europe: Tibbets." *Asian Political News* 12 August 2002. http://www.findarticles.com/p/articles/mi_m0WDQ/is_2002_August_12/ai_90297071/print. Accessed 8 August 2006.

Van Orman, Edward. "One Thousand On Top: A Gunner's View of a Flight from the Scanning Blister of a B-36." *Air Power Magazine* January 1987.

Wachsmuth, Wayne. *B-36 Peacemaker.* Waukesha WI: Kalmbach Publishing, 1995.

"Weapon Storage Sites: Q Areas." http://www.globalsecurity.org/wmd/facility/q_area-intro.htm. Accessed 30 March 2006.

"Weapons of mass destruction (WMD). B-36 Peacemaker." http://www.globalsecurity.org/wmd/systems/b-36-design.htm. Accessed 29 March 2006.

"Weapons of mass destruction (WMD). Mark 4." http://www.globalsecurity.org/wmd/systems/mk4.htm. Accessed 29 March 2006.

Welch, John. *RB-36 Days at Rapid City.* Rapid City SD: Silver Wings Aviation, 1994.

"What Have We Done?" 6 August 2005. http://www.kanenas.net/index.php?entry=entry050806-142432. Accessed 8 August 2006.

"Winston Churchill's Iron Curtain Speech." http://www.history1900s.about.com/library/weekly/aa082400a.htm. Accessed 8 August 2006.

Wolk, Herman. "The Blueprint for Cold War Defense." *Air Force Magazine* March 2000.

—— "Revolt of the Admirals." *Air Force Magazine* May 1988.

—— "The Battle of the B-36." *Air Force Magazine* July 1996.

—— "The New Look." *Air Force Magazine* August 2003.

"XB-36, Giant Bomber Undergoing Ground Tests." *Science Newsletter* 6 July 1946.

Index

Numbers in italics refer to illustrations and photographs.

C

G

H

I

J

K

N

O

P

Q

R

S

T

NORMAN S. LEACH IS A CANADIAN HISTORIAN, FREELANCE WRITER, PROFESSIONAL speaker and adventurer. A graduate from the University of Manitoba, he majored in Strategic Studies and minored in Canadian History. During this time he began to focus his interests on Canadian military history. Norman is the author of *Great Military Leaders* and *Canadian Peacekeepers*. In *Broken Arrow*, he continues to write on military history and asymmetric warfare. A regular contributor to *Canadian Defense Review* Norman is an active member of the Winnipeg Press Club and travels the world in the search of story and book ideas.

Norman lectures on military issues, including both historical and modern topics. Recent addresses have included "Vimy Ridge and Canadian Sovereignty," "The Evolution of Peacekeeping: Cyprus to Afghanistan" and "Bosnia: A Story of Canadian Peacekeeping."

An avid military collector, Norman is recognized as an expert on British and Commonwealth Cavalry militaria and is often consulted by collectors, historians and museums from around the world. He was the official historian for *Passchendaele*, a Paul Gross movie filmed in Calgary in 2007.

Norman's contributions to his community and the Canadian Armed Forces have earned him several honorary titles and awards, including the Canada 125 Medal, the University of Lethbridge Crystal Award and the Alberta Centennial Medal for outstanding contribution to community service. He is an Honorary Peacekeeper and was a director of the Canadian Forces Liaison Council. Currently, he is an Honorary Commander of the Military Museums in Calgary and is a serving member of both the Mounted Forces Commemorative Troop and the Legion of Frontiersmen. He and his wife, Maritza, reside in Calgary, Alberta, with their two daughters.